German Influences IN
LOUISVILLE

EDITED BY C. ROBERT ULLRICH AND VICTORIA A. ULLRICH

THE
History
PRESS

Published by The History Press
Charleston, SC
www.historypress.com

Front cover, top: *Courtesy C. Robert Ullrich and Victoria A. Ullrich.*
Front cover, bottom: *Courtesy Lewis A. Meyer.*

First published 2019

Manufactured in the United States

ISBN 9781467144070

Library of Congress Control Number: 2019944029

In memory of Martha Elson.

CONTENTS

FOREWORD

To leave behind one's homeland, family, friends and culture is a difficult decision. Then, to travel on a perilous journey across a vast ocean and start life anew in a foreign land certainly must be a stressful situation. This is what thousands of German immigrants did in the nineteenth century. Enduring this anxiety-filled experience resulted in many achieving their hopes of a brighter future.

My German ancestor, John Jacob Wiser, stowed away on a ship at age twelve. He settled in southwest Jefferson County, married Luzanna Arnold, had nine children and owned a four-hundred-acre farm. John's life paralleled those of many other Germans whose fortitude and hard work resulted in a prosperous existence for them and their many descendants.

From construction workers, carriage makers and blacksmiths, to jewelers, photographers, artists and musicians, among many other skilled craftsmen, Germans built a successful society in Louisville—far away from their native country. No matter where one goes in our city, there is most likely a German connection to that location. In neighborhoods like Germantown and Butchertown, as well as in numerous churches, schools, medical services and businesses, there are references to German immigrants who helped those places to be established and flourish.

This book celebrates all these men and women of German heritage who overcame the challenges and established new lives in Louisville. It documents their legacy of meaningful contributions. There are very few books about the German influences on our city, and this book greatly expands on this understanding.

Louisville greatly benefited from the knowledge and determination of German immigrants to create a community that is now one of the best places to live in America.

Stephen A. Wiser, President
Louisville Historical League

ACKNOWLEDGEMENTS

The editors would like to thank everyone who contributed to this book, especially the chapter authors. Also, we would like to acknowledge the invaluable assistance of John E. Kleber and Mary Jean Kinsman, who served as manuscript editors.

Special thanks are due to Reverend R. Dale Cieslik of the Archdiocese of Louisville Archives for his generous help as well as the University of Louisville Photographic Archives and the Filson Historical Society for the use of their collections. Finally, the editors would like to thank the many individuals who contributed photographs from their personal collections for use in this book.

Chapter 1

INTRODUCTION

BY C. ROBERT ULLRICH AND VICTORIA A. ULLRICH

Although Pennsylvania Dutch settlers lived in Louisville as early as the 1780s, the first German-born immigrant to arrive here was August David Ehrich, a master shoemaker from Königsberg, Prussia, who came in 1817. The first Louisville city directory, published in 1832, included Ehrich and twenty-four other German-born heads of household, including John Schmidt and Emanuel Seebold, who emigrated in 1819.

In contrast to the small number of Germans living in Louisville in 1832, the German immigrant population of Louisville in 1840 was at least four thousand, and the neighborhood east of the city center, known as Uptown, was completely populated by Germans. Similar dramatic increases in the German populations of Cincinnati and St. Louis occurred in this same time period. There are two main reasons for this.

First, following the Napoleonic Wars (1803–15), the Congress of Vienna established the German Confederation, a loose association of 39 kingdoms, duchies, principalities and free states. While the Confederation was essentially the same alignment of states that existed before the wars, most Germans had hoped for national unity instead. By the 1830s, the lack of a coherent economy in the German states, coupled with political unrest, led to disillusionment. Many Germans seeking new opportunities saw the United States as an enticement. Unrest in the German states continued through the 1840s, culminating with the 1848 Revolution, which also failed to unify Germany and led to another wave of immigration to the United States. The wave of immigrants that came to the United States in the 1830s, known as the

The German Confederation, 1815–66. *Courtesy Wikimedia Commons.*

"Dreissigers" or "Thirtiers," numbered as many as all of the Germans who had come in the colonial period. Whereas only 5,753 Germans immigrated to the United States in the 1820s, 124,726 came in the 1830s and 385,434 came in the 1840s.

Second, Robert Fulton's *New Orleans*, built in Pittsburgh in 1811, was the first steamboat on the Ohio and Mississippi Rivers. Very few steamboats were built to operate on the Ohio River before 1820 but by 1834, 304 had been built in Pittsburgh, 221 in Cincinnati and Covington and 103 in Louisville and Jeffersonville. The advent of the steamboat coincided with the first significant wave of German immigrants to arrive in the United States, and it enabled immigrants to move from ports of arrival in the East to the interior of the country via the inland waterway system. As a result, cities along the Mississippi and Ohio Rivers, such as Evansville, Louisville, Cincinnati and St. Louis, experienced a significant influx of German immigrants in the 1830s.

One reason that immigrants chose Louisville was the Falls of the Ohio River. Prior to the construction of the Louisville and Portland Canal in 1830, boats traveling upstream unloaded passengers and cargo at the Portland Wharf, located several miles northwest of Louisville. Anyone wishing to continue traveling upstream would journey on land to Louisville and board another boat at the Louisville Wharf. Of course, the reverse was true for passengers traveling downstream. Many immigrant passengers simply stayed in Louisville rather than traveling on. Even after the canal had been built, both Portland and Louisville remained important stops for travelers along the Ohio River, and many immigrants disembarked at the Falls and settled in Louisville.

In German immigrant enclaves along the Ohio and Mississippi Rivers, many immigrants wrote letters home, encouraging others to join them in America. And they did. From 1850 through World War I, 5 million German immigrants came to America, with 1.5 million of them arriving in the 1880s.

Sketch of the Portland Wharf near its peak of steamboat activity in 1853. *Courtesy University of Louisville Photographic Archives.*

Nearly 7.5 million Germans immigrated to the United States from 1820 through 2010—by far the largest number of any nationality.

By 1850, Germans and their families represented one-third of Louisville's population. German immigrants founded ethnic churches in Louisville as early as 1836, and by the end of the Civil War there were eight German Protestant churches, seven German Catholic churches and two German Jewish congregations. The first German-language newspapers in Louisville were published in the 1840s. By 1850, every brewery in the city was German-owned. A German lending bank was established in 1854, and trades and industries all flourished under German ownership. Germans were engaged in the legal and medical professions as well as the fine arts and music. In 2010 according to the federal census, one-third of Louisville's population claimed German ancestry.

The chapters of this book were chosen to illustrate how German immigrants influenced Louisville's growth and culture. The chapter topics range from the 1848 Revolution in Germany, which brought radicals and free thinkers to the United States and Louisville, to a series of profiles of German immigrants who arrived in Louisville in the twentieth century. Post–Civil War Catholic churches are examined as well as the strong Protestant Evangelical movement in Louisville. Other chapter topics include financial institutions, large industries, small trades and even the German involvement in mineral water and soft drink bottling. Finally, the strong German presence in southern Indiana is featured in all aspects, including churches, industry and trades.

Readers should note that in this book immigrants from the various German states that became part of the unified German Empire in 1871 are called "Germans." German-speaking immigrants from areas outside the German Empire, including those from Austria, Bohemia and parts of Switzerland, are identified by their nationalities.

Chapter 2

GERMAN RADICALISM
AND THE FORTY-EIGHTERS

By John E. Kleber

Every European immigrant who came to America brought something to the melting pot. In the mid-nineteenth century, Germans composed an increasingly large number of those immigrants. As they boarded ships in Bremen, Hamburg, Rotterdam and other ports of embarkation, they carried tangible possessions such as clothing and money—the number and value depending on the individual. Less tangible were the varied skills such as farming or trades. Even less tangible were each person's unique ideas that were formed in the environment of the Old World. Some came with liberal ideas. Among those was a small group of German radical intellectuals known as the Forty-Eighters. As with their possessions or skills, their idealism enriched the melting pot and contributed significantly to American thought.

Between 1803 and 1815, Europe was ravaged by the Napoleonic Wars. At its end, Prince Metternich of Austria established a new balance of power, called the Concert of Europe, at the Congress of Vienna. This restored monarchies, reflected conservative principles and prevented widespread European war for a century. A German Confederation was formed, replacing the Holy Roman Empire and including thirty-nine states with a federal Diet. By the middle of the century, most of Europe lived under regimes of political repression, autocratic governments and aristocratic privilege. But by then, the system was beginning to fray, and republican principles—a heritage of the French Revolution—started to stir among the middle class and in the minds of intellectuals. Revolution was brewing across Europe, born of hope and discontent with the status quo.

Richard Wagner noted, "Europe appears to us as a high volcano," and it spewed forth as the Revolution of 1848. It began in France in February when Louis Philippe was deposed, and a Second Republic was established. Almost immediately, Germany was infected with calls for constitutional change and reform. From an advanced age Metternich observed, "I am an old doctor; I can distinguish a passing illness from a mortal ailment. We are in the throes of the latter." To make matters worse, a cholera plague ravaged Europe through the summer and fall of 1848 and appeared shackled to the violent popular uprisings.

The history of the revolution in Germany is complex and open to varied interpretations. Prussia was one of the most powerful German states, and in March 1848, with a sense of nationalism in the air, there were riots in Berlin where three hundred were killed. This left a legacy of bitterness. Although workers' societies sprang up in many German cities, they did not result in a revolutionary dictatorship by the workers. They were simply unprepared to assume control of the government. Instead, it was hoped that a constitutional monarchy would bring reform. The Prussian king was Friedrich Wilhelm IV, who assumed the throne in 1840. He proved to be a romantic, mystical, artistic, idiosyncratic man who believed he knew what was best for his people. Shocked by the riots, he initially gave in to limited reform but bided his time as the revolution played itself out.

Important to German liberal thought was the idea of a constitution. The idea had been present in Europe since the ratification of the United States Constitution. The drafting and writing of a constitution lay in the hands of delegates elected to a national assembly in Frankfurt. Almost six hundred representatives, mostly lawyers, wealthy landowners and members of the upper middle class, met at the Paulskirche on May 18, 1848. From the beginning, there were significant divisions and competing ideas.

They set about their work: "the product of a moral idea, of reason, logic, sentiment, and of a desire for a better order of government and society." Issues of nationalism, internationalism and republicanism were debated. The work resulted in endless litigating until it seemed to be only an assembly of professors who lacked the instinct for power and the capacity for cooperation. Members were discovering it was easier to overthrow the past than to construct the future. Ahead of their time, they failed to carry a majority of people with their republican view.

They persevered, however, and completed a constitution on March 27, 1849. A copy was sent to Friedrich Wilhelm with an offer of the crown of a greater Germany. Soon after he refused it on April 28, the Frankfurt

Above: Berlin riots, March 1848. *Courtesy Wikimedia Commons.*

Right: Friedrich Wilhelm IV. *Courtesy Wikimedia Commons.*

Session of the Frankfurt Parliament, June 1848. *Painting by Ludwig von Elliott.*

Parliament collapsed, and the constitution was never implemented. But what they wrote shook up German society and, for a time, held some of the strongest European powers at bay. It would later resonate in the United States among Forty-Eighters and in the Louisville Platform.

It was a remarkably modern document that reflected the idea of greater freedom. Section one laid out the geographical boundaries of the Reich. Section two listed the rights of the Reich Authority and the individual German states. Section three made the head of the Reich an Emperor with limited powers. Section four defined the nature of the Reichstag and defined its powers. Section five established a Supreme Reich Court. Sections six and seven guaranteed the basic rights of the German people. It recognized all Germans as equal before the law, provided free elementary education to all, abolished serfdom, protected property, granted the right to assemble, demanded representative voice in taxation and impeachment, gave the right to vote to every person at age twenty-five and established free expression, faith and conscience.

Hanna Ballin Lewis, a best-selling German writer, was in Frankfurt. At the end of 1848, she pondered, "And now, in this hour, I ask myself:

what will the coming year bring to us?" After a brief period of optimism, it brought renewed control of the European continent by conservative forces, as revolutions were crushed with brutal force.

Heinrich Heine observed, "A revolution is a tragedy, but an even greater tragedy is an unsuccessful revolution." It was this failure that propelled many revolutionaries to immigrate to a more amenable land where their ideas would be more in tune—to a freer and more democratic society—that land was the United States. Of the thousands who fled Germany, some were escaping punishment while others were escaping dissatisfaction with political conditions. Among them were "not only hundreds of professors, poets, musicians, artists, editors and professional men," but many simple artisans, shopkeepers, farmers and laborers as well. A small number would be known as Forty-Eighters. Frederick Bogen noted in 1851 that it was a great blessing when German immigrants stepped on American shores. Bogen said, "He comes to a free country; free from the oppression of despotism, free from privileged orders and monopolies, free from the pressure of intolerable taxes and imports, free from constraint in matters of belief and conscience."

Some of these political refugees came to Louisville. They found not only a political system similar to their own ideas of a democratic national republic but a city of growing prosperity and population. In 1850 with a population of 43,194, it was the fourteenth largest city in the United States and "seemed well-equipped to meet whatever challenges the new decade might offer." Work was easy to find in a growing manufacturing sector. In the 1850s, $4 million was invested in manufacturing—much of it in small enterprises, and there came to be fifteen iron foundries. But economic life was still found along the Ohio River, where in one day forty-five boats were in port. During the decade, an astonishing 25,000 immigrants came to live here, among them the Forty-Eighters. German neighborhoods were established, especially east of the downtown. For the first time, there were German schools, churches, newspapers and a Turnverein.

The beer gardens were indicative of the Germans' appreciation for more than just labor. In those gardens and over steins of beer, Germans debated the politics of the day. No one debated more ferociously than the Forty-Eighters, who considered themselves more exile than immigrant. In his book *The German in America*, Frederick Bogen offered a wide range of practical advice to German immigrants. He warned against "too great excitement and fanaticism in matters of politics and religion." While he understood the desire of those who had suffered under oppression to exercise their newfound freedom, he feared they would regard liberty as "nothing more or less than recklessness, or the privilege of doing as he pleases." His call for placing duty before looking out for the rights of man sometimes fell on deaf ears. This was especially true among those Louisville Germans who formed the Bund Freier Männer (League of Free Men) in 1853 and who in the next year proclaimed the goals of "Liberty, Prosperity and Education for All," which were principles of the German Revolution.

The party was a vehicle for the Forty-Eighters to bring their radical ideas to the American melting pot. While they believed themselves to be upholding the same principles found in the Declaration of Independence and the Constitution, nativists (those who were born in the United States and opposed foreign influences) had another view. Terming the Forty-Eighters malcontents and worse, they formed the American Party (Know-Nothings) to counteract, among other things, this German influence. One principal objection was to the Louisville Platform, which was published in 1854. It summarized the core outlook and demands of the German American radical Democrats. It began with a statement of what was wrong with the United States and suggested reforms in an alliance between liberal Germans and progressive Americans. It advocated ideas such as the abolition of slavery, direct elections and equality between men and women. In that regard, there is a similarity between the Louisville Platform and the Frankfurt Constitution. Apparently first published in *Der Pionier* in March 1854, it was reprinted in some thirty German-language newspapers and was widely debated.

Five names were attached to the Louisville Platform. Among them was Karl Peter Heinzen, who founded *Der Pionier* and was its publisher for twenty-five years. He made it "a progressive manifesto critical of many aspects of life and government in the United States." Born in Grevenbroich in the Rhineland-Palatinate, he was a known intellectual and a long-time critic of the Prussian government. By 1845, he was engaged in socialistic writings. When the revolution was suppressed, he fled to the United States and settled in Louisville, where he brought forth the principles of radical Germans and became one of the best known Forty-Eighters.

Heinzen and the other signatories invited a discussion of the Platform "without narrow-minded nativism and blind party spirit." However, it was not to be. Reaction was swift and divided, and the Platform was supported by only a small number of Germans and almost no nativists. This surprised its writers, who felt its changes would enforce principles promulgated in the founding documents of the United States by more fully democratizing government processes, structures and policies.

"We have no other interests than those of the American people...because the interest of the American people is the interest of the whole human race," wrote a supporter.

Nativists disagreed, claiming the Louisville Platform had nothing in common with American principles of government or social organization. Written by men of "delicate hands" who lacked sufficient knowledge of the English language to read the laws of the land, they feared it would demolish long-established customs and institutions. One nativist tract stated, "To become an American citizen and a voter, a man should have been born and educated among us. He will then have some chance of understanding the nature of our institutions,

Karl Peter Heinzen. *Courtesy Max Kade Institute for German-American Studies, University of Wisconsin-Madison.*

and the working of our system. He will have no foreign prejudices to get rid of. He will have no foreign preferences to forget. He will have no foreign ignorance to be enlightened."

In Louisville, the backlash constituted part of the anti-immigrant feeling at mid-century. It contributed to the Bloody Monday riots of August 6, 1855, when at least twenty-two people were killed, mostly German and Irish immigrants. In some ways, this mirrored the violence against the revolutionary ideas that occurred in Europe in the 1850s.

The Forty-Eighters, men of principle and action, may have been ahead of their time. In the short term, they failed to carry out their ideas, but in the long term, their principles proved right. Historian G.M. Trevelyan said, "1848 was the turning point at which modern history failed to turn." That may be true, but it was Germans who spoke early and clearly for the republican democracy so dear to the heart of Americans. In doing so, Jacob Mueller felt they brought "the positive qualities of the German character to bear on the process of developing America," and they laid the foundation "for a free and respected German community" in Louisville and the United States.

Chapter 3

POST–CIVIL WAR GERMAN CATHOLIC CHURCHES

By William C. Schrader

The Diocese of Bardstown/Louisville initially included the entire state of Kentucky, but in 1853 the Diocese of Covington was created for the eastern part of the state, and in 1937 the Diocese of Owensboro was created for the western regions. After that time, the Archdiocese of Louisville (so elevated in 1937) only covered the central portions of the state. Catholics in the archdiocese are primarily found in the so-called "Kentucky Holy Land" of Nelson, Marion and Washington Counties as well as Louisville/Jefferson County.

At the time of the Civil War, Germans and their families represented about one-third of the population of Louisville. Though there were more German Catholics than Irish Catholics in Louisville, from 1868 to 1924 the diocese was dominated by the Irish under Bishops William George McCloskey (1868–1909) and Denis O'Donaghue (1910–1924). Finally, in 1924 Louisville got its first German bishop, John Alexander Floersh (1924–1967), who also became the first archbishop in Louisville in 1937. This ethnic rivalry shows in the composition of the delegation sent by the diocese to the Catholic Congress at Chicago, held in association with the Columbian Exposition in 1893. The roster began with the name Edward McDermott and included Irish names, as well as names from historic Maryland families of central Kentucky, but the list did not include a single notable German.

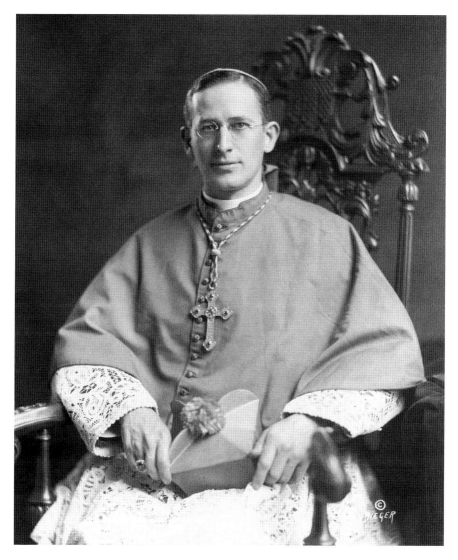

Archbishop John Alexander Floersh. *Courtesy University of Louisville Photographic Archives.*

In addition to their participation at the parish level, though, German Catholics had an impact at the diocesan level and beyond the Catholic community. The Louisville diocese had a German Catholic newspaper, the *Katholischer Glaubensbote*, published from 1869 to 1914. For many years, its editor, Edward Neuhaus (1844–1910), was considered the most prominent German Catholic in town. The *Louisville Anzeiger* was published from 1849

Monsignor George William Schuhmann. *Courtesy Archdiocese of Louisville Archives.*

to 1938, and while not specifically Catholic, it contributed to the spread of information among the German Catholic population. Its last editor, Richard Schuhmann, also was a prominent German Catholic.

Richard's brother, George William Schuhmann, was also a prominent Louisville Catholic of German heritage. George was born in 1865, the eldest of nine children, and died in 1931. He obtained a doctoral degree from the University of Innsbruck and lived in Europe for seven years. In Louisville, after serving as a priest at the Cathedral of the Assumption and as pastor at St. John's, he was appointed as chancellor of the diocese in 1910. Between the death of Bishop O'Donaghue and the installation of Bishop Floersh, he served as apostolic administrator before he was appointed by Floersh as vicar general. He held this dignity until his death. George Schuhmann served in many public capacities: member of the board overseeing the diocesan newspaper, *The Record*, member of the Catholic Orphans Board; member of the mayor's Vice Commission and member of the Louisville Free Public Library Board, among others. He was especially involved in service to the poor, and the Schuhmann Social Center located at 730 East Gray Street is named in his honor.

During the period prior to the Civil War, Catholics of German background established a flourishing community in Louisville. Five German parishes, St. Boniface (1837), Immaculate Conception of St. Mary (1845), St. Martin of Tours (1853), St. Peter (1855) and St. Joseph (1866), were founded in less than thirty years. In 1866 there were eleven parishes in the area that would become the historic city of Louisville prior to the adoption of metropolitan status in 2003. In addition to the Cathedral of the Assumption and St. Michael, which had no specific ethnic identity, were the Irish parishes of St. Patrick, St. John and St. Louis Bertrand as well as the French parish of the Church of Our Lady (Notre Dame du Port). From this enumeration, it is clear that German Catholics made up about half of the Catholic population of the city.

After the Civil War, German Catholic numbers continued to grow. While immigration continued, and the membership in existing Catholic parishes increased, the original five parishes were soon swamped. This resulted in the establishment of six new parishes in the period between the Civil War and World War I. These were St. Anthony of Padua (1867), St. Vincent de Paul (1878), Holy Trinity (1882), St. Francis of Assisi (1886), St. Elizabeth of Hungary (1906) and St. Thérèse of Lisieux (1906). It is remarkable that St. Anthony was Portuguese, St. Vincent was French, St. Francis was Italian, St. Elizabeth was Hungarian (although married to a German), and St. Thérèse was French—not a German among them. The Catholic Church is, after all, catholic.

The first of the new parishes after the Civil War was St. Anthony of Padua, the twelfth parish established in Louisville. This parish was formally established in 1866 on property at Twenty-third and Market Streets that was purchased for $490, but it did not become active until the following year. St. Anthony was established to serve the German Catholics living west of Fifteenth Street. After a difficult beginning, the parish was entrusted to the administration of Reverend Bonaventure Keller, Order of Friars Minor Conventual (OFM Conv.), who was the pastor at St. Peter's. The first Franciscan assigned as pastor of St. Anthony's was Reverend Pius Kotterer, OFM Conv., two years later. He invited the Franciscan Sisters of the Third Order Regular from Syracuse, New York, to take charge of the school.

Under the fourth pastor, Reverend Louis Miller, OFM Conv., the present church building was constructed, with the cornerstone laid on May 18, 1884, and consecrated on May 22, 1887. The bells in the steeple were imported from Bochum in Westphalia.

In 1899 the Franciscan sisters were succeeded by the sisters of the Order of St. Ursula, and the first Ursuline principal was Sister Ambrose. Until the outbreak of World War I, classes at St. Anthony Parochial School were taught in both German and English, and many prayers, hymns and sermons were given in German. During the 1930s, a drum and bugle corps was organized at the school by Mr. Raymond Kalaher and won many prizes in citywide competitions. The parish was visited by the great flood of 1937, followed by a fire in 1939 that left the parish in dire straits. It was not until the 1950s that the parish fully recovered.

The second German ethnic parish founded after the Civil War was St. Vincent de Paul, which was formed from the southern part of St. Martin of Tours parish in 1878. The original St. Vincent de Paul church building was located at the corner of Milk (Oak) Street at what was known as Chester Avenue (now an alley) in the present Shelby Park neighborhood. The first pastor was Reverend Herman Henry Plaggenborg, a diocesan priest. At that time, the area was undeveloped and contained many fields and ponds, and

St. Anthony Catholic Church after the fire of 1939. *Courtesy St. Anthony Church Centennial Volume, 1967.*

the initial membership was only about one hundred families. As part of the foundation ceremonies, the parish witnessed a mission by Passionist priests who preached in German in the morning and English in the afternoon. When few people came to the English sermons, they were abandoned, and German alone was used. Once the parish was operational, the regular sermons and hymns were in German as well.

Under the second pastor, Reverend John H. Heising, who served from 1879 to 1900, great strides were made in developing the parish. In 1886, the cornerstone was laid for the present church building. When the church was blessed by Bishop McCloskey in 1888, the sermon was preached in German by Monsignor Francis Zabler, pastor of St. Martin of Tours. Membership continued to expand, necessitating the establishment of two new parishes in 1906—St. Elizabeth of Hungary, with 300 families, and Holy Trinity (now St. Thérèse of Lisieux), with 250 families. Despite these divisions, by 1928, the fiftieth anniversary of the founding of the parish, it became necessary to expand the church of St. Vincent de Paul from a seating capacity of 800 to 1,300.

The original school associated with St. Vincent de Paul was founded by Reverend Plaggenborg and entrusted to the Sisters of Charity, but after only two years, the school was moved to the Sisters of St. Ursula, who were more prepared to teach classes in German. The second school building was constructed in 1911, during the pastorate of Reverend Andrew J. Thome, on the southwest corner of Shelby and Oak Streets. After an addition in the 1920s, the school accommodated about 850 children. That structure is now the Maloney Center of the Archdiocese of Louisville, an office complex and the site of the archdiocesan archives.

In rural Jefferson County to the east of Louisville, in the later nineteenth century, the city of St. Matthews was established and named for St. Matthew Episcopal Church. Rail service began in 1851, and with a stop in St. Matthews, some found it convenient to live there and commute to work in Louisville. In 1880 Nanz and Neuner (now Nanz and Kraft) Florists established the first major commercial business in the community. In 1882 Bishop McCloskey established a new parish to serve the Catholics in this area, which was named Holy Trinity. This parish mostly consisted of about 500 people from families of Swiss and German derivation who worked in the agricultural areas and small businesses. The first pastor was Reverend Louis C. Ohle, formerly the pastor at St. Vincent de Paul in Louisville. Ursuline sisters were brought to staff the school upon its opening shortly after the parish was started, and German was a language of instruction into the early twentieth century. In 1899 a book was published in German to celebrate the jubilee year of the St. Joseph Orphans Society. It described Holy Trinity as "ideally located" and consisting of 110 families with eighty children in the school. From 1925 to 1938, the parish was served by priests of the Congregation of the Most Precious Blood but was staffed by diocesan clergy. Growth continued at a slower pace during the Depression and war years but expanded greatly thereafter. A new church structure was completed in 1953, and the original land on which the parish was located became the campus of Trinity High School.

The fourth new German ethnic parish in the Louisville area was St. Francis of Assisi. This parish is located in the southeastern part of Louisville, on Bardstown Road. It was established by Bishop McCloskey in 1886 and entrusted to the first pastor, Reverend Bernard Westermann. Only forty-five families made up the parish at that time. In the following year the school was begun with Sisters of Mercy as teachers. Shortly thereafter, the sisters of the Order of St. Ursula succeeded them. Under pastor Theodore Reverman, a new school building was constructed and dedicated in 1925. A new church

Aerial view of St. Elizabeth of Hungary Catholic Church. *Courtesy St. Elizabeth of Hungary Parish Fiftieth Anniversary Volume, 1956.*

building was planned, but because of the Depression and the war years, the building was not completed until 1952.

On December 12, 1905, Reverend James J. Assent, an assistant at St. Martin of Tours, received a letter from Bishop William George McCloskey, commissioning him to establish the parish of St. Elizabeth of Hungary on property already acquired on Burnett Avenue—southwest of the parish of St. Vincent de Paul. The church and school were dedicated on September 2, 1906. In the first year, two hundred students enrolled and were taught by the Ursuline sisters. Within the next four years, the rectory and convent were built. The cornerstone of the present church was laid on August 9, 1914. Under Reverend James F. Knue in the 1920s, the school's enrollment grew to more than one thousand. In 1933, the first sons of the parish to be ordained were Pax Schicker, OFM, Bernard Spoelker, William Borntraeger and C.J. Weiker, whose family names indicate the continuing German ethnic nature of the parish.

The last of the German ethnic parishes was initially dedicated to the Holy Trinity. In 1906 this parish was established in the Germantown/Paristown neighborhood on the corner of present Kentucky Street and Schiller Avenue. The founding pastor was Reverend Peter Berresheim, a German immigrant from Andernach on the Rhine River. On September 9, 1906, at the opening of the parish school, Reverend Berresheim, five Ursuline sisters and 145 children were present for the opening Mass. As there was not yet a church building, the Mass was held at St. Vincent de Paul Church, and everyone then marched a few blocks to the temporary school at 1063 East Kentucky Street. In January 1907, the new school building opened, and in February 1908, the original church building was dedicated. In 1929 the second pastor, Reverend Andrew Zoeller, and Archbishop Floersh presided over the dedication of the new church building. The name of the parish was changed in recognition of the prior claim to the name Holy Trinity by the parish in St. Matthews. (By this time, the city of St. Matthews was considered to be part of greater Louisville.) The Holy Trinity on East Kentucky Street became the parish of St. Thérèse of Lisieux, who had been canonized on May 17, 1925, even as the earliest plans for the new structure were being discussed. The church of St. Thérèse was dedicated to a French saint, designed in the Spanish Colonial style and served a German ethnic congregation.

From the schools associated with these parishes, it is clear that the German ethnic parishes were best served by the Sisters of St. Ursula. They were first brought to Louisville from Straubing in Bavaria in 1858 by Reverend Leander Streber, OFM, the first pastor of St. Martin of Tours. Even though

St. Therese of Lisieux
Catholic Church. *Courtesy
Archdiocese of Louisville Archives.*

other orders were first invited to teach at several of the schools, they soon gave way to the sisters of the Order of St. Ursula.

After World War I, sermons and classroom instruction were no longer given in German. In the next generation, families moved to the suburbs, and ethnic neighborhoods were broken up. After World War II, it is inaccurate to speak of German ethnic parishes in Louisville, there was only an ethnic heritage.

Chapter 4

THE GERMAN EVANGELISCH MOVEMENT

BY REVEREND GORDON A. SEIFFERTT

Martin Luther posted his Ninety-five Theses on the Wittenberg church door on October 31, 1517. Thus began the Lutheran contribution to the Protestant Reformation of the Christian Church. By 1522, in Zürich, Switzerland, Ulrich Zwingli initiated what became known as the Reformed contribution, which gave rise to other groups such as the Presbyterians and Congregationalists. Luther and Zwingli attempted to unite their Reformation movements at the Marburg Colloquy in 1529. Because they agreed on many issues but disagreed on others, they went their separate ways.

Over the next centuries, the Reformation leaders and theologians continued their unification movement efforts with no success until Friedrich Wilhelm III became the king of Prussia. He was a devoted member of the Reformed church and was married to Queen Louise, a Lutheran. Fervor for union was increasing in his kingdom, so he decreed that Lutheran and Reformed would become one—Evangelisch—derived from the New Testament Greek *euangelion*, meaning "gospel" or "good news." The king declared the edict effective on October 31, 1817, exactly three hundred years after Luther's Ninety-five Theses. This was the first, and one of the few, unions of two differing movements in Christian Church history. Other German principalities also adopted the Evangelisch union.

The Evangelisch movement sought ways to be at one with other Christians in terms of ministry to the world. Thus, the first mark of the Evangelisch was the conviction that most important for Christians was not their creeds, which divide Christians, but their actions—loving God, loving others and doing good unto others. The second mark of the Evangelisch was to work together to care for the least—the orphans, the elderly and the sick. The third mark, thoroughly inclusive and ecumenical, was to seek unity, or at least cooperation, among Christians. An old motto, which fit them well, is, "In essentials, unity. In nonessentials, liberty (diversity). In all things, love."

German speakers flocked to the United States over the centuries, and in the 1800s, Evangelisch settled in cities from the East Coast to the Midwest to Texas. The first Evangelisch church in the United States was established in New Orleans by the 1820s. Its first members were indentured servants who sold their services for transport to these shores.

The first Evangelisch arrived in Louisville by the early 1830s and established The First German Evangelical Church of Louisville, Kentucky, in 1836. It became St. Paul German Evangelisch Church, building twice on Preston Street at Green (Liberty) Street and later moving to Broadway. St. Paul's second pastor, Karl Daubert, assisted with the establishment of St. John Evangelisch Church in the Market-Hancock Streets area in 1843 and St. Peter Evangelisch Church in 1847, where Central High School is now located. By 1900, Louisville was home to eight Evangelisch congregations.

Though small in number in the United States, by 1920 the Evangelisch had established ten orphanages, fifteen homes for the elderly, nine hospitals, two homes for the "Epileptics and Feebleminded" and a mission house in a poverty-stricken area of St. Louis. In Louisville, the Evangelisch were instrumental in the establishment of an orphanage (which became Brooklawn), a home for the elderly (the Altenheim) and eventually a hospital (Methodist Evangelical Hospital). These Evangelisch ministries are illustrative of this movement's ethos.

Its pastors, especially two Louisville pastors, are also indicative of the Evangelisch spirit. Karl (Charles) Ludwig Daubert was born in 1801 in Hirzenhain, Darmstädtischen Oberhessen, and studied at the University of Strasbourg. He arrived in the United States in 1826 and was ordained in Philadelphia's Salem Reformed Church. By 1840, he was a pastor in Quincy, Illinois. Daubert responded to an invitation to come to a gathering of Evangelisch-minded pastors in 1840 near St. Louis. He was one of the five original signers and the president of the Deutsche Evangelische Kirchenverein des Westens (German Evangelical Church Society/Fellowship of the West). From 1841 until retirement in 1874, he was the pastor of Louisville's St. Paul Evangelisch Church.

For Evangelisch Karl Daubert, the past was never a straitjacket constraining the present and the future. The past was foundation for

Right: Reverend Karl Daubert.
Courtesy Bethel-St. Paul Church.

Below: German Protestant Orphan
Asylum. *Courtesy University of
Louisville Photographic Archives.*

responding in the present and building for the future. The 1830s German immigrants had grandchildren, and even great-grandchildren, who could probably speak and understand the German language, but who were also living in an English-speaking culture. The forward-thinking Daubert had to plan for the eventual assimilation of German immigrants into American society.

A growing number of German Protestant orphans needed care. Daubert was instrumental in establishing such a home in 1851. Some wanted it to be just a St. Paul's ministry, while others wanted it to be named "Evangelisch." Daubert and others, exhibiting the Evangelisch movement's spirit, successfully made it far more inclusive, and it became the German Protestant Orphan Asylum.

Seldom in church history is a pastor of another church, much less of another denomination, remembered. But in the 130th anniversary volume of First Lutheran Church on Broadway (originally, First English Lutheran Church) is this statement: "Father Daubert, the pastor of the church at Preston and Green, came to help us lay that corner stone. He was the only one of the German Pastors that favored us in any way. The others were indifferent."

Louisville's St. Luke Evangelisch Church history records that "Daubert put forth many noble efforts to unify Germans of the city into congregations." He helped establish St. Luke's and before that St. John's. He even made the difficult journey to Evansville for the dedication of that city's St. John Evangelisch Church in 1852.

Daubert also built St. Paul's, which included a parochial school. The 1848 city directory states that the congregation had "1,000 communicant members," by far the largest non–Roman Catholic church in the city. The church edifice, built in 1860 during his pastorate, was a magnificent structure.

According to the city directories of the 1860s, Daubert was far ahead of his time in offering two German and two English worship services each Sunday—German at the prime times (10:00 a.m. and 7:30 p.m.) and English at 8:30 a.m. and 1:30 p.m. In the 1872 city directory, the English services were at the prime times.

Theophilus "Ted" Friedrich John was born in St. Louis on July 30, 1866, into a family of at least four generations of pastors, including two of his brothers. He was educated in his father's church's parochial school and then the Evangelisch pro-seminary in Elmhurst, Illinois, and its St. Louis area Eden Seminary. All of his schooling would have been in the German

Reverend Theophilus John. *Courtesy St. John United Church of Christ.*

language, but he lived his whole life in an English-speaking culture. He was both excellently bilingual and bicultural.

John pastored St. John Evangelisch Church from 1898 to his unexpected death in 1912, shortly after his daughter, the third child, was born.

During his tenure, St. John's assisted with ministry to orphans, the elderly and the sick. When the German Protestant Orphan Asylum moved from its initial location on West Jefferson Street near Twentieth Street to a new location between Bardstown Road and Baxter Avenue (the location of the present Mid-City Mall) in 1903, St. John's provided financial and organizational backing. Soon after his arrival at St. John's, Miss Mary Rothenberger and her Good Will Circle responded to the need for elder care. In 1906 they established the Louisville Protestant Altenheim on Barret Avenue, south of Breckinridge Street, where it still resides.

In Germany, Evangelisch and other Protestants established orders of Deaconesses, which were unmarried women called to particular ministries. In the United States, the Evangelisch Deaconess motherhouse was in St. Louis. Their primary ministries were children, the ill and the elderly. Pastor John and St. John Church, with participation by other Evangelisch congregations, had several Deaconesses ministering to the ill before 1910. A goal, finally realized in 1960, was the opening of Methodist Evangelical Hospital on Broadway.

St. John's Young People's Circle (YPC) began a few years before John's arrival, but it only had 13 members. Six months after his arrival, it had 259 members and by 1903 there were 467 members. The YPC gave a magnificent stained glass window and a Chickering grand piano, among many other gifts, to St. John's. The YPC provided the complete outfitting for the girls' infirmary in the German Protestant Orphan Asylum's relocation.

Obviously, John related well with the young people, but he also related with the older Germans. In the church archives is a photograph taken at a church picnic of John and two much older men who are absolutely beaming at their pastor.

St. John Evangelical Church interior. *Courtesy University of Louisville Photographic Archives.*

In the early 1900s, the church finally paid off the debt for the sanctuary built in 1867. The church building was then thoroughly refurbished, and a new spire was built on the steeple, replacing the original one.

Because John was bilingual, he could pray, lead worship, preach and converse easily in either language. During his tenure, English worship services moved from Sunday evenings to occasional Sunday mornings, then to most Sunday mornings. Confirmation classes were in English, in addition to German, and as the decades went by, more and more classes were in English.

In 1906 when the school house was demolished, a Parish Hall was constructed. It was not just for church activities, as the second floor became a public auditorium that could seat more than 570 people. The audience's chairs were placed on a floor sloping toward the stage for improved viewing, and the stage had a slight slope toward the audience. Even today, a ticket booth remains across from the auditorium's entry doors. During the construction of the Parish Hall, the YPC was preparing Gilbert and

Sullivan's *Mikado* with eighty in the cast. The production packed the old Macauley Theatre and repeated to a full house at the new Masonic Theatre.

The Evangelisch in the United States produced an English version of its German hymnal. Pastor John and St. John Church chose instead the Northfield Hymnal, an American hymnal that included hymns not only from its German tradition, but also well beyond.

During his tenure, John led St. John Evangelisch Church to become the preeminent German Protestant Church and a leading German cultural center in Louisville.

The Illinois-Missouri Evangelisch produced three of the twentieth-century Protestant theological super-stars: brothers Reinhold and H. Richard Niebuhr and their sister Hulda Niebuhr.

The Evangelisch were born of the very rare event of parts of two strands of Christianity merging into one in 1817. Unity was in their genes. The Evangelisch and the German Reformed in the United States merged in 1934 to become the Evangelical and Reformed Church. In 1957 that group merged with the 1931 merger of Congregationalists and another strand of the Christian tradition, to become the United Church of Christ.

Cooperation and close relationship to other Christian groups has continued from the 1817 Evangelisch union through the present United Church of Christ. The Evangelisch movement has been very involved with local, state, and national councils of churches during the past century. One Great Hour of Sharing, which provides disaster relief around the world and locally, has been significantly supported by the Evangelisch movement since its beginning, following World War II. In Louisville, New Albany and Jeffersonville, congregations influenced by the Evangelisch movement have been instrumental in the establishment of the neighborhood ecumenical ministries that blanket this metropolitan area.

From 1817 to the present and into the future, the spirit of the Evangelisch movement ministers to the least and provides an enriching and enabling yeast of inclusion and ecumenicity within the Christian community in Louisville and far beyond.

Chapter 5

FINANCIAL INSTITUTIONS

By R. Charles Moyer

In May 1780, the Virginia Assembly passed an "act for Establishing the Town of Louisville." During that year, three hundred families arrived in Louisville, and a man named John Sanders established Louisville's first financial institution. Sanders accepted the skins of fur-bearing animals from pioneers and gave them "certificates of deposit" as receipts. These certificates circulated much like a currency and were used in trade. When the furs were sold, the certificates were called in and paid off. This first bank was located at Third and Main Streets.

Other banks were established in succeeding years to support the commercial development of Louisville. By the early 1850s, Germans and their families accounted for one-third of the city's population. Austrians, Swiss and Alsatians added to the German-speaking population. This rapid growth of the German population may be traced, in part, to the unsuccessful protests and rebellions that took place in Germany in 1848. The middle- and working-classes in Germany grew discontented with the aristocratic and autocratic governance in many of the thirty-nine independent states of the German Confederation. The Revolution of 1848 ended unsuccessfully for the liberals, and many of them were forced into exile to avoid persecution. Large numbers of these exiles found their way to Louisville. With the rapid increase in Louisville's German-speaking population, it is not surprising that German financial institutions would develop to serve the growing immigrant population.

GERMAN INSURANCE COMPANY

In 1854, the German Insurance Company was incorporated. The founders of the company were primarily successful merchants, and a majority of the founders were of German origin or descent. The original charter of the company not only granted the authority to provide insurance services, but it also granted considerable banking authority. The charter was amended in 1860 to give the company even broader banking authority. In 1872 state banking laws were changed, requiring the separation of banking and insurance operations. The banking part of the original firm became known as the German Insurance Bank. In 1887 the bank had capital of $249,500 and deposits of $1,489,000. By 1918, the bank's deposits had grown to $5,660,470.

In the years following the granting of its charter, there was substantial turmoil in the United States' financial markets that led to the failure of many financial institutions. But the German Insurance Company, through prudent management and strong leadership, was able to sell its stock and begin operations.

The first bank president, Jacob Laval, was of French descent, and his primary business was distilling and dealing in liquors. The bank declared

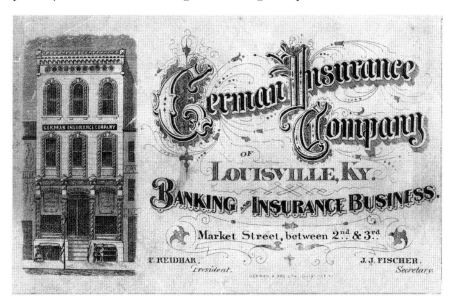

German Insurance Company advertisement. *Courtesy Louisville City Guide and Business Directory, 1869.*

its first dividend of 10 percent at the end of 1859. In 1862 Franz Reidhar, born in Switzerland in 1807, was elected as the first full-time president of the German Insurance Company. He served from 1863 until 1889. Mr. Reidhar came to the United States in 1834, arriving in New Orleans, and traveling to Louisville on a boat that landed in Portland, Kentucky—then a separate city from Louisville. He found work helping to restore a wrecked steamboat, worked in a store, established a thriving bakery in Jeffersonville and began a successful clothing business in Louisville. When he sold the clothing business, he made large investments in the German Insurance Company. Mr. Reidhar was a shrewd businessman and investor, and he died wealthy and respected.

The original office of the bank was at the northeast corner of Fourth and Market Streets. In the early 1860s, the bank moved to Third Street between Main and Market Streets, and in 1868, plans were completed for a three-story brick and stone building located at 231 West Market Street. This building served the bank and insurance company well until 1887, when the bank moved to an elegant and larger headquarters structure at 207 West Market Street. The new headquarters of the bank featured a distinctive clock tower that remains one of Louisville's important landmarks.

With the arrival of World War I, many in the German community of Louisville, and elsewhere in the United States, sought ways to downplay their German heritage. In 1918 the German Insurance Bank changed its name to Liberty Insurance Bank. Its sister insurance company, the German Insurance Company, changed its name to the Liberty Fire Insurance Company. Other financial institutions followed suit, including the German Security Bank, which became the Security Bank, the German-American Bank and Trust Company of New Albany, which became the American Bank and Trust Company, and the German Bank, which became the Louisville National Bank.

GERMAN NATIONAL BANK

The German National Bank was organized and chartered in 1872 at 101 West Market Street. Between 1872 and 1897, the bank issued a total of $981,730 of national bank notes in various denominations. In 1887 the bank had capital of $251,500 and deposits of $672,000.

After operating successfully into the early 1890s, the bank was impacted by the recession of 1893. In 1889 there were ten national banks and twelve state banks in Louisville. Under the pressure of business failures during the recession, by 1895 those numbers declined to seven national banks and nine state banks. Although the German National Bank survived the 1893 recession, it was a troubled institution. On January 18, 1897, the German National Bank was placed in the hands of the Bank Examiner's office.

At the time of its failure, the bank had $251,500 of capital and a recorded surplus of $81,000. The bank's tenuous financial condition was largely the result of the failure of the Louisville Deposit Bank. Its investment in Louisville Deposit Bank cost the German National Bank $75,000. Lawsuits involving between $250,000 and $300,000 were pending, arising from the German National Bank's connection to Louisville Deposit Bank. Between January 2 and January 15, 1897, the bank experienced deposit withdrawals of approximately $75,000. The run on deposits was reported to the controller of the currency, who ordered the bank closed immediately. On January 22, 1897, the president of the bank, Mr. J.M. McKnight, was arrested and prohibited from having any further association with national banks. In February, Mr. McKnight was further charged with conspiracy to defraud the bank.

GERMAN BANK

The German Bank was originally incorporated as the German Bank and Insurance Company of Louisville and was chartered on March 16, 1869. The banking department and the insurance department were separated in 1870. In 1887 the bank had capital of $800,000 and deposits of $1,503,000. The bank occupied its new Beaux-Arts style headquarters at Fifth and

German Bank, about 1939. *Courtesy University of Louisville Photographic Archives.*

Market Streets in 1914. In 1918, the German Bank changed its name to Louisville National Bank, joining other German financial institutions in downplaying their German origins. By 1918, the bank's deposits had grown to $4,147,337.

GERMAN SECURITY BANK AND INSURANCE COMPANY

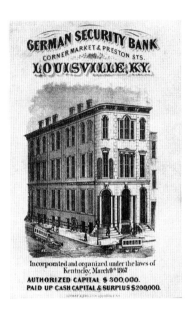

Incorporated and organized under the laws of Kentucky, March 9th 1867
AUTHORIZED CAPITAL $ 300,000.
PAID UP CASH CAPITAL & SURPLUS $200,000.

German Security Bank advertisement. *Louisville City Guide and Business Directory, 1869.*

The German Security Bank and Insurance Company was a successful early banking institution in Louisville. It was chartered in 1867, largely through the efforts of James B. Barrett. Mr. Barrett was born in Munfordville, Kentucky, and came to Louisville at the age of sixteen. He was first employed as a store clerk and rose to be a partner in the firm by 1855. In 1863 he became a partner in the largest retail dry goods establishment in the city. He remained in this role until he obtained the bank charter to provide a bank located in the heavily German Uptown section of Louisville. He served in the role of cashier of the bank for the balance of his career and died in 1910.

The bank opened for business in May 1867, in a building that had previously been a barbershop. The original charter of the bank was broad, permitting the "buying and selling of promissory notes, stock and bonds, other securities and things, together with issuing policies of insurance on all kinds of property and things against loss, damage or injury from any cause whatever."

In 1911 the bank moved to an elegant new Greek-revival limestone building at the northeast corner of Preston and Market Streets. The original capital stock of the bank was $100,000 but that was increased to $179,000 in March 1869. In 1887 the bank had capital of $179,000 and deposits of $739,000. By 1918, the bank's deposits had grown to $990,000.

WESTERN GERMAN SAVINGS BANK

Ernest Christian Bohné. *Courtesy Filson Historical Society.*

In 1872 the Western German Savings Bank was organized, and its founder, Ernest Christian Bohné, became the bank's cashier. Ernest Bohné was born on February 4, 1840, in Hessen-Kassel. His father was a publisher and bookseller and served as an officer in Napoleon's army during the Russian campaign from 1810 to 1812. Bohné left school at the age of fourteen and began to learn the book trade. He soon tired of this work and went to sea, landing in New Orleans in 1856. He immediately found his way up the Mississippi and Ohio Rivers and settled in Louisville. He worked in a dry goods store and served in the Civil War as a quartermaster sergeant. In 1862, he took a position as office manager and bookkeeper at the Louisville Hotel. In 1872 he organized the Western German Savings Bank and became the cashier. Bohné was known as a brilliant and insightful banker and often addressed the banking community on important banking issues of the day. Perhaps, more importantly, Bohné was a leader in Louisville's civic affairs. He served as a school trustee for three years and as a charity commissioner from 1877 to 1880. His most lasting impact on the Louisville community began in 1891, when he became a member of the first board of park commissioners. He played a leading role in selecting the sites for Cherokee and Shawnee Parks and in commissioning the development of the parks to Olmsted and Company.

The Western German Savings Bank was originally located at Ninth and Market Streets. In 1874 the bank was reorganized and renamed the Third National Bank of Louisville. In 1876 the bank moved to the southwest corner of Fourth and Market Streets. Bohné remained as cashier of the bank until 1905, when he moved to a position at Southern National Bank. In 1887 the Third National Bank had capital stock of $300,000 and deposits of $525,000.

GERMAN AMERICAN BANK

By 1895. the German banks in Louisville had capital totaling $1,480,000, or 17 percent of the total of bank capital stock in the Louisville market. By 1918, only one bank in the area retained the word "German" it its name. A latecomer to the German heritage bank scene in the region was the German American Bank, organized on November 2, 1910. The flagship bank of German American Bancorp was the German American Bank in Jasper, Indiana. Jasper is a small town in southern Indiana about two hours west of Louisville. The town of Jasper, barely a century old in 1910, was settled mainly by German immigrants.

The founder of the bank was William F. Beckman, a local civic leader and the county's treasurer. The initial capital stock was $40,000, subscribed to by fifty-seven initial stockholders. The bank opened on December 19, 1910, and had just two employees. It now has branch offices in the Louisville region, including Jeffersonville, as well as branches in New Albany, Indiana, and Carrollton, Kentucky. In late 2017, the bank had total assets of $3.064 billion and total deposits of $2.444 billion. The bank did not follow the lead of the German heritage banks in Louisville that removed the "German" name from their banks.

INSURANCE COMPANIES

In addition to the banking institutions mentioned above, German financial institutions also organized a number of insurance companies, including German Insurance Company of Louisville (1869), German Security Insurance Company (1867), Falls City German Mutual Fire Insurance Company (1884), German Mutual Fire Insurance Company of Jefferson County (1874), German Washington Mutual Fire Insurance Association (1860) and Louisville German Mutual Fire Insurance Association (1856).

Chapter 6

MANUFACTURING

By Gary Falk

German immigrants made countless contributions to the creation of manufactured products in Louisville and southern Indiana. A review of historical documents quickly reveals the ingenuity and creativeness of these individuals and the success of their enterprises. From musical instruments to textiles, and from leather goods and machinery to icehouses, it is fascinating to see how varied the stories are. The sketches provided below are only a sample of the many contributions German immigrants made to Louisville.

THE ALBERTS FAMILY

John Bernard and Clara Burman Condermann Alberts emigrated from Germany to the United States in 1885. John was born in Munster, Westphalia, in 1854. He and his wife arrived in New York and spent one year in Memphis and three years in Cincinnati before moving to Louisville. John, along with Louis Lussky, started the firm Alberts and Lussky Art Glass Company, which was located on the southeast corner of First and Market Streets. Their business was billed as "designers and decorators in stained and mosaic art glass, specializing in churches, private and public buildings." John Alberts installed art glass in scores of Louisville buildings and in other structures throughout the United States, including New York. In Louisville, his work may be seen in St. Brigid Catholic Church

Gisbert Alberts. *Courtesy University of Louisville Photographic Archives.*

and in the First Christian Church. John Alberts died in 1926 and is buried at St. Michael Cemetery.

John Alberts and his children also had a fascination with raising flowers, namely cultivating orchids at his home at 129 Galt Avenue in Crescent Hill. Worldwide fame came to the Alberts family, especially son Gisbert (1893–1992) and daughter Elinor (1898–1938), in the industry of growing orchids. Elinor perfected some 48,000 baby orchids and began selling them to florists throughout the United States. In 1927, the family purchased fifteen acres of land at 4318 Westport Road, where they ultimately built seven greenhouses. From these greenhouses, they were able to maintain 50,000 blooming plants and 50,000 in the seedling stage. Elinor became an acknowledged world expert in orchids and became the head of the Orchid Department at the Missouri Botanical Garden in St. Louis in 1926. By 1930, she had 60,000 hybrids thriving in her laboratory. To this day, she is recognized as an important part of the garden's history.

Elinor married David Hunt Linder, a professor of botany at Harvard University, in 1928. She passed away at age forty in 1938 in Boston. Gisbert Alberts continued to operate the Alberts Orchid Company until his retirement in 1974. He died at age ninety-eight in 1992. Both Gisbert and Elinor are buried in Cave Hill Cemetery.

DURLAUF MUSIC SHOP

The Durlauf Music Shop was a fixture in Louisville for sixty-four years. The store was located at several sites in downtown Louisville—in the 600 block of South Fifth Street, 312 West Broadway and 658 South Fourth Street—as well as at two sites in St. Matthews.

The seeds were sewn for a life of music when Michael Floren Durlauf, his wife, Ursula, and their infant son, Michael Jr., emigrated from Bavaria in 1858 and settled in Jasper, Indiana, a small town populated mostly by first- and second-generation German families. Michael Durlauf was a stone carver by trade but was also a musician and band leader. Both of these talents served him well. He made his first mark on his new country by serving as an "expert snare drummer" in the 49th Regiment of the Indiana Volunteer Infantry in the Civil War.

Michael Durlauf Jr. (1856–1931) followed in his father's footsteps as a stone carver and musician, but he also became an established architect and contractor. He married Jasper resident Elizabeth Gutzweiler, whose parents were also German immigrants. In 1894 Michael Jr. designed the Dubois County Soldiers' and Sailors' Monument, which stands on the courthouse square in Jasper. He designed many of the buildings on the campus of Jasper College, and he carved many of the gravestones in Jasper's St. Joseph Church cemetery.

Michael and Elizabeth had six sons and two daughters. Their son Leo (1880–1954) was a well-known trombonist and stone carver. He moved to Louisville and played trombone at the old Macauley Theatre and was elected as the president of the Musician's Union Local 11 in 1935. Another son, Frank (1893–1984), was a well-known draftsman who moved to California and worked for Hal Roach Studios, Warner Brothers and CBS. A third son, Alexis (1889–1952), who played drums and composed music, moved to Louisville and worked at the Macauley, National, Strand, Mary Anderson and Brown theaters.

In 1926 Alexis (Alex), along with Tom Barry, opened a music store named Durlauf-Barry Music, where they sold violins, cellos, trumpets and crank phonographs. After a short time, Barry opened his own store, which marked the beginning of the Durlauf Music Shop. When Alex died in 1952, his sons, Max and Dick, operated the business. When Max died in 1976, Dick, along with other family members, operated the store. It was a business that spanned three generations.

The Durlauf Music Shop filled a niche in the (mostly) acoustic musical instrument trade of Louisville. Professional musicians traveling through the city patronized the store for instruments and accessories. The store offered repair services and had a staff

Alex Durlauf. *Courtesy Durlauf Collection.*

of fine musicians who taught students. The Durlauf shop was also a center for "networking" among local musicians. Over time, Durlauf's amassed a huge collection of photographs of musicians and music venues.

Trends in music changed drastically with the emergence of rock and roll. Bands from the time of the original immigrant Durlauf family became less popular, and brass and woodwind instruments, which formerly dominated theater and night club music, were gradually replaced by electronic instruments. Many venues that once featured live bands switched to recorded music, and the cost of maintaining a "brick and mortar" facility became increasingly difficult to bear. Durlauf's closed in the late 1980s, but to those musicians who still remember the shop, it represents a time and place where they could share their craft and advance their profession.

ICEHOUSES

With ready access to ice today, it is hard to imagine how precious it was as recently as a hundred years ago. The average citizen faced many difficulties to acquire and maintain ice for food preservation and long-term storage. Even ice cubes for cold drinks were all but a dream.

The process of transporting and using ice in the United States involved a number of steps—locating frozen ice sources, converting the ice into manageable and transportable sizes and weights, loading the ice and distributing it throughout the country with minimum loss, unloading it at special warehouses, further cutting and sawing it into marketable sizes and reloading and transporting it to local jurisdictions. The logistics of ice harvesting and distribution were daunting, to say the least.

All of these considerations changed with the invention of artificial ice, which offered two main advantages over natural ice. First, the source of the ice was clean, potable water, not water from a stagnant pond. Second, the ice manufacturing process was local, and it was not necessary to transport or store ice harvested from distant sources.

The first commercial machines creating "plant ice" emerged in the 1880s. Ice machines, first based on ether or ammonia absorption, creating so-called tube ice, were inefficient, but the technology improved over time. Several large manufacturing companies in Louisville produced artificial ice using these machines. Henry and Adam Vogt, whose parents emigrated from Freinsheim in the Rhineland-Palatinate, manufactured ice machines in

Louisville at the turn of the twentieth century. Their company, Vogt Ice, is still in business but no longer has a local manufacturing presence.

There were many ice companies in Louisville and southern Indiana throughout the nineteenth century and early twentieth century, and many of the pioneers in this trade had connections to Germany. One of the first natural ice companies in Louisville was the Northern Ice Company, established in 1855. They delivered ice to steamboats, hotels and homes. Their product was frozen lake water. The three operators of this company, at different times, were George Skinner, G. Gosnell and Eli Vansickle.

Another early natural ice business was that of Louis (born c. 1819), and Peter Hammer (c. 1827–1873), who came to the United States from Bavaria. Both were listed in the 1860 census as ice traders in Louisville. John T. Monsch (1811–1884), who was born in Germany, established offices in Louisville and New Albany with his Northern Lakes Ice Company in 1864. Perhaps the earliest company to market plant ice in Louisville was the Pictet Artificial Ice Company of New York, which arrived in Louisville in 1881.

The Rohrman family played a prominent role in the early marketing of manufactured ice in Louisville. John Rohrman (1863–1932) started with

Grocers Ice and Cold Storage Company, 1937. *Courtesy John E. Kleber.*

the Northern Lakes Ice Company, but in 1894 he founded the Rohrman Ice Company as an artificial ice manufacturer. Rohrman became known as "The Ice King." His company's offices were at 518 Third Avenue, and the factory and cold storage facility were at Fourteenth and Magazine Streets. His brother, Benjamin Rohrman (1877–1958), was the superintendent of the well-known Arctic Ice Company, which was located in various places throughout the city. The Rohrman brothers were born in Louisville, but their parents were German immigrants.

Mathias Poschinger, a native of Germany, established the Louisville Ice Company in 1894 and was the president and founder of the New Albany Ice Company. He also served for a time as the president of the Grocers Ice and Cold Storage Company at 609 East Main Street and was involved with ice-making machinery as the president of the American Machine Company at 510 East Main Street.

It is important to note the smaller distributors of ice, both natural and manufactured, who served small neighborhoods in Louisville. These companies, some of which sold meat and other products in addition to ice, were part of the fabric of the ice trade. One such company was the Forcht Ice Company in Louisville's West End. William Forcht (1842–1917), a butcher, immigrated to the United States from Hamburg. He set up a small shop near Thirty-fourth and Herman Streets about 1889. His son, Oscar H. Forcht, converted the store into an icehouse in 1925, eventually passing it along to his two sons, Oscar C. and Calvin A. Forcht. It remained in the family for several generations.

MADAME GRUNDER

Christina M. Johnson (probably an Anglicized surname) was born about 1846 in Hannover, Germany. Her family immigrated to the United States and settled in Louisville before 1860. While still a teenager, she started her dressmaking business in a small house on East Green (Liberty) Street and displayed a tin sign outside marked "Dressmaking." In 1873 she married Louisvillian George Grunder and became "Madame C. Grunder."

Madame Grunder's business grew rapidly, and before long, she moved to an address on South Fourth Street above a salon named Hupe's Hair Store. Eventually, she moved to the Tyler Building and finally to the Bernheim Building in the 600 block of South Fourth Street.

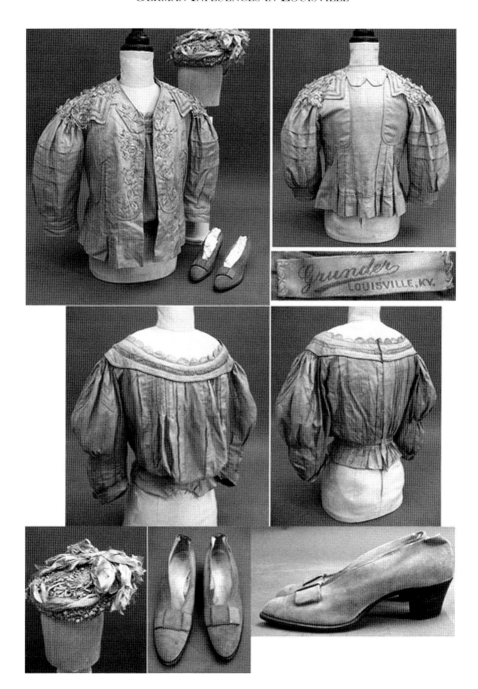

Madame Grunder clothing items. *Courtesy Holly Jenkins-Evans.*

Madame Grunder operated her dressmaking company for sixty years. In her busy season, she was known to hire more than one hundred women to work in the shop. She made all types of women's clothing, especially wedding dresses, fashion dresses and specialty dresses. Her dresses became known worldwide, and she frequently traveled to Europe to purchase fabrics and trims for her many products. In her travels she became closely associated with the great French dressmaking firm, House of Paquin, and grew to be close friends with Jeanne and Isidore Paquin. Her company catered to many dignitaries, making dresses for the wives and daughters of governors, mayors and senators.

Madame Grunder died in 1920 at the age of seventy-four. Her business survived until at least 1930, and from 1923 until 1928, it was managed by Olive G. Todd at the Bernheim Building facility.

Christina M. Grunder is buried in Cave Hill Cemetery.

PRANTE ORGAN COMPANY

There were a number of piano and organ manufacturers in Louisville in the nineteenth century, and many of the founders of these companies had strong ties to Germany and the German organ building tradition.

Pump organ and piano maker Cyrus Adler, the largest builder of keyboard instruments in Louisville, was of German-speaking heritage, as both of his parents were immigrants from Bohemia. The piano company founded by Julius Hinzen and Ernest Rosen in the mid-1800s made outstanding pianos with hand-crafted cabinets. Both emigrated from Germany to the United States, and many of their instruments still survive. More recently, pipe organ builder Gottfried C. Reck, of the Louisville firm Steiner-Reck, emigrated from West Germany to the United States in 1966.

August Prante and his pipe organ company was another such example. He was born in 1844 in Prussia and immigrated to the United States with his parents, Joseph and Philomena, and sister, Mary, in 1852. The family lived in various places before settling in Louisville by 1856. Joseph Prante (1812–1897) was a cabinet maker who later became a pipe organ builder. His firm eventually became August Prante & Son and remained in the family until 1909. Prante organs were installed throughout the United States and were common in Louisville. The organs in St. Boniface Catholic Church (1891), St. Joseph Catholic Church (1894), St. Peter Evangelical

Prante organ at St. Philip Neri Church. *Courtesy Organ Historical Society.*

Church (1895) and St. Philip Neri Catholic Church (1899) were all built by the Prante organ company.

In all, three generations of the Prante family worked in organ building and repairing. They also did woodworking, and evidence exists that they made hunting rifles. At various times, family members were found in Kentucky, Indiana and Ohio, undoubtedly based on various organ building projects.

One of the earliest pipe organ installations done by the Prante family was for the church in Ferdinand—near St. Meinrad, Indiana—in 1856. For many years thereafter, the Prante family had strong ties to the area surrounding St. Meinrad, where Joseph Prante maintained a shop at Second and Main Streets.

The first instance of the Prante firm in the Louisville city directory was in 1858, in which Joseph Prante was listed as an organ builder on the north side of Green (Liberty) Street. In the 1860 census, he was listed as a cabinetmaker. By 1866, after an absence of several years from the Louisville city directories, Joseph was listed with shop and residence at 91 West Jefferson Street. By this time, his company was largely associated with his son, August, although some evidence exists that Joseph was still working in the trade. Several city directories in southern Ohio in the years following 1866 showed Joseph living in Cincinnati and Chillicothe. Joseph Charles Prante died in Louisville in 1897. His funeral was held at St. Martin of Tours Church, but he was interred at St. Margaret Cemetery in Chillicothe.

August Prante was listed in the Louisville city directory as an independent organ builder in 1867, with a shop and home address on Market Street at the southwest corner of Twentieth Street. His company was listed as the "Louisville Organ Manufactory, August Prante, Proprietor." In subsequent years, he was listed at several addresses in that area. By 1874, August and his family had moved to St. Meinrad, Indiana, to build organs in that area—much as his father had done earlier. August remained in St. Meinrad as an organ builder until 1889, then moved to Owensboro, Kentucky, where he was listed in city directories as a "manufacturer of pipe organs" and as a "repairer and tuner of organs and pianos." August returned to Louisville by 1891, when he was listed in the city directory at 1820 West Market Street. His company later moved to a vacant church building at 538 Roselane Street at the southwest corner of Hancock Street. From 1896 forward, his business was listed as "August Prante & Son."

August Frederick Prante died in an unfortunate runaway buggy accident at Broadway and First Street in Louisville in 1900. At the time, his firm was moving the organ from the old St. Boniface Church to the newly-constructed church at Green (Liberty) and Jackson Streets. He is buried at St. Michael Cemetery in Louisville.

QUAST SHOE MANUFACTURING COMPANY

In the history of Louisville, there have been at least twenty-one shoe manufacturers. During the peak years of shoe production, from 1875 to 1925, there were four major shoe factories, producing more than thirty-five hundred pairs of shoes daily. In 2019, there is only one shoe manufacturer in

Quast Shoe Manufacturing Company letterhead, 1906. *Courtesy Gary Falk.*

Louisville—Kleinman's Living Shoes. Kleinman's produces specialty shoes on a one-by-one basis, but virtually all other shoes sold in the United States are made overseas.

One of the major shoe manufacturers in Louisville's history was the Quast Shoe Manufacturing Company, first known as the Quast and Schulten Shoe Company, founded in 1867 and located at the northeast corner of Sixth and Main Streets. Quast later manufactured at this site, with a specific division called the Louisville Boot Factory. The Quast factory was founded by John H. Quast (1843–1919), whose parents, Franz and Wilhelmine, came to the United States from Germany in the mid-1800s. John Quast's two sons, Frank W. (1873–1920) and Carl F. (1882–1958), were both active in the company. The Quast shoe factory was located at 1446–1448 Levering Street in an industrial corridor of the city south of Magnolia Street and west of Sixth Street. The site of the Quast factory, about two acres, is now an open field.

The Quast factory—one of the most advanced of its day—was built 50 feet by 175 feet and four stories tall in 1905. Quast had a daily output of more than two thousand pairs of shoes with about 125 employees and 7 salesmen, who covered thirteen states in the southern and midwestern United States. The company flourished until the early 1920s, but in 1926, they were deemed bankrupt.

The Quast Shoe Company brands included Ben Hur, Mammoth Cave and Big Brother for men, as well as Bluegrass Belle for ladies. For children they had a Gladmore brand. Their shoes were all leather, and their motto was, "If you handle good shoes made of good leather, Quast Quality Shoes will be of value to you, otherwise our line will not interest you."

Chapter 7

MINERAL WATER, SOFT DRINKS AND THE MUNICIPAL WATER SUPPLY

By Peter R. Guetig and Conrad D. Selle

Although a method for infusing water with carbon dioxide was developed by Joseph Priestley in 1767, the commercial manufacture of carbonated water did not begin until the late eighteenth century. Soda water, carbonated water and seltzer water all refer to water infused with carbon dioxide. Soda water flavored with fruit or spice flavors and sweetened is generally called a "soft drink" or "pop." Mineral water and soft drinks were commonly consumed before the municipal water supply was developed rather than drinking water from possibly contaminated wells.

MINERAL WATER

Mineral waters from various springs and wells were consumed for their therapeutic value, as they were purported to cure or alleviate ailments such as constipation, dyspepsia, rheumatism, gout, kidney disorders, liver disease, diabetes, tuberculosis, syphilis and nearly every other sort of complaint. Imitations of famous European waters were made by adding small quantities of various chloride, carbonate and sulphate salts of magnesium, sodium, potassium chloride, etc. Commercially sold mineral water was often artificially carbonated.

The first city directory listing for soda and mineral water in Louisville was Dr. James W. Garrison, a local druggist, in 1836. Most druggists were soda manufacturers and had soda fountains in their drugstores. There were about as many drugstores as saloons—one on every corner. They were popular places for young men to take young women on Saturday night dates. By 1859 there were five druggists listed in the city directory, but there were probably more based on the number of recovered 1850s vintage bottles.

By 1881, *The Industries of Louisville* listed six mineral water manufacturers with a total capital of $15,200, employing an average workforce of 12 male adults and 2 children, working ten hours a day with wages from $1 to $2 per day to produce $26,693 worth of products. By comparison, the local cooperage industry was listed as having $361,300 in capital with an average workforce of 543 and produced products worth $762,800.

As indicated by the 1881 statistics, most local bottling firms of this period consisted of two or three men, often the partners of the firm, siphon-filling the bottles by hand. Soda bottles were made of thick glass due to the high level of carbonation, and wired-down corks were used for capping. Only a few hundred bottles could be filled in a day. Between 1890 and 1910, large-scale production became possible with the advent of crown capping, modern bottling line machinery and automatic bottle washers. Better sanitation and

Soda water bottles. *Courtesy William Lindsey, Klamath Falls, Oregon.*

quality standards, plus the influence of the temperance movement, made soft drinks increasingly popular.

The mineral water bottling firm of W. Springer began in 1873 and operated until 1939 under the name Springer Brothers. Joseph Renn of New Albany began bottling in 1870, and his son, Joseph Renn Jr., operated a bottling business in New Albany until 1947. Other mineral water manufacturers were Ernest Heinecke, Paul Hanes, Heinecke and Weber, Lauer and Brand, H.G. Prenger and Company, Jacob Ruckstuhl, Jacob Schanzenbacher, G.H. Schmidt, A.D. Schmitt, H. Schuckman, George Stang and Charles Goss.

From 1836 to the beginning of the twentieth century, 101 companies in Louisville were either bottling natural water or manufacturing mineral water. From 1900 to 1925, there were fifty-five additional companies, and since 1925, there have been many more.

SOFT DRINKS

Through most of the nineteenth century, soft drink manufacturers lasted only a few years, but several local companies with larger operations lasted well into the twentieth century. In the early 1900s, several local beverages were popular, including Teapho, Rivo-Cola, Mel-Ola and Parfay, to name a few. Herman Epping, a German immigrant, founded a soft drink manufacturing firm in 1863 that was continued by his son, John G. Epping. The Epping firm, a major local soft drink manufacturer into the 1960s, produced Seven Up, Kentucky Club Ginger Ale, Orange Crush, Epps-Cola, Epping's Grape and Lemon Sour. In the late 1930s, the Epping Company also operated branch plants in New Albany, Campbellsville and Lexington and used a fleet of forty trucks to deliver their products. The former Epping plant was purchased by Pepsi-Cola General Bottlers in 1967 for $1.3 million and included franchises for Seven Up, Orange Crush and Like Cola. Their plant buildings were located on the northwest corner of Logan Street and Broadway and are still standing.

At the beginning of the twentieth century, franchised beverages began to be manufactured in Louisville. As well as being bottled there, soft drinks were marketed at soda fountains. The local Coca-Cola bottling plant was begun in 1901 by Fred S. Schmidt at 1008 West Main Street. It was the second Coca-Cola franchise in the United States—the first

John G. Epping Bottlers. *Courtesy University of Louisville Photographic Archives.*

was in Chattanooga, Tennessee. The plant purchased syrup from the parent company, diluted it and bottled it. Coca-Cola distributed syrup for fountain drinks through a separate company, in some degree competing with the bottled product. The Coca-Cola bottling plant was moved to larger quarters at Sixteenth and Bank Streets in 1912 and to a much larger plant at 1661 West Hill Street in 1941. Bottling was discontinued in 1991 when the company had about four hundred employees. A large number are still employed in distributing operations.

Pepsi-Cola was first bottled in Louisville in 1937 by Pepsi-Cola Louisville Bottlers, Inc. The plant at 1500 Algonquin Parkway, built in 1942, employed a workforce of 130 when it was acquired by Chicago-based Pepsi-Cola General Bottlers Inc. in 1956. A new plant was built at 4008 Crittenden Drive in 1957. Bottling at the Louisville plant was discontinued in 1991, though distribution operations still continue.

Dr. Pepper Bottling Company of Kentucky also operated a plant at 2340 Frankfort Avenue from 1937 to 1979.

Royal Crown began bottling in Louisville in 1946 and is the only soft drink bottler remaining in Louisville. Their plant is located at 6207 Strawberry

Lane. In 1995 Royal Crown had about 165 employees and produced fifteen million cases of soft drinks. In 1962 Royal Crown introduced Diet Rite, the first nationally distributed diet soft drink.

This process of bottling at large regional plants and using former bottling plant sites as distributors is a national trend in the soft drink industry.

Following the pattern of breweries in other parts of the United States, Falls City, Oertel and Fehr breweries were notable entrants to the field of local soft drink manufacturing during the Prohibition period. All enjoyed considerable success in soft drink manufacturing but quickly dropped their soft drink lines to resume the manufacture of beer after Prohibition was repealed in 1933. One Oertel soft drink, Say Tay, was designed by the brew master and contained cinnamon and yerba mate, a South American herb widely used to flavor beverages.

The Renn family operated a bottling business on State Street in New Albany, Indiana, for seventy-five years—first bottling ale, porter, stock ale and lager beer, as well as mineral water and soft drinks. There were several other soft drink bottling operations in New Albany.

Falls City soft drinks. *Courtesy University of Louisville Photographic Archives.*

Today, Pepsi-Cola is bottled nationally by PepsiCo. Seven Up, Dr. Pepper, Canada Dry, Orange Crush, Nehi and Royal Crown are bottled by The Snapple Group, an integrated refreshment beverage business marketing more than fifty beverage brands throughout North America. Coca-Cola is bottled by the Coca-Cola Consolidated Bottling Company.

MUNICIPAL WATER SUPPLY

Before the installation of a municipal water supply in Louisville in the late nineteenth century, illness and death from contaminated water was prevalent. Many people preferred the relative isolation of country living, being further removed from the bad water, communicable diseases, bad sanitation and horrible smells of the city, with wells or cisterns in every backyard. Water could be boiled for tea or coffee, or inhabitants could drink beer, wine or whiskey.

In the 1830s and 1840s, Louisville was known as the "graveyard of the west," largely due to the poor quality of the water. The population of Louisville reached 43,154 in 1850, and the problems of poor water quality had gotten even worse. Frequent epidemics of cholera, typhoid, dysentery and other diseases broke out from polluted water. On March 6, 1854, the Kentucky Legislature decided to form the Louisville Water Company. It was to be a private company, but after only 55 shares were sold privately, the voters approved 5,500 shares in 1856 and another 2,200 in 1859, making it almost wholly state-owned. An elegant, state-of-the-art water tower was built on River Road and began operation on October 16, 1860, with a capacity of twelve million gallons per day and twenty-six miles of pipe.

In *The Quest for Pure Water*, the Louisville Water Company noted that water obtained by pumping the Ohio River was far from perfect: "In 1860, Louisville Water customers could fill a glass with water and let it sit so the mud would settle to the bottom…but taking water from the Ohio River was better than drinking from a contaminated well."

In 1819 Henry McMurtrie wrote in *Sketches of Louisville and Its Environs*,

> *The well water of Louisville, which is found at various depths from sixteen to forty feet, and which is the one commonly used by the inhabitants, is extremely bad, containing, besides a considerable quantity of lime, a large*

Louisville Water Tower. *Courtesy Library of Congress.*

portion of decomposed vegetable matter…the water of the wells, after standing a little time, becomes nauseous to the taste and acquires a smell highly disagreeable to delicate stomachs…. This bad quality of the water in general use is one great cause of a variety of complaints, particularly diarrhea, that are so common in the summer months, and calls loudly for a remedy, which can be found in the steam engine and the Ohio, whose waters being extremely pure, might with a little expense, be distributed through every part of town, an arrangement which will probably take place at no very distant period.

Louisville Water Company Chief Engineer Charles Hermany began advocating for treating river water shortly after Louisville Water began delivering drinking water. Hermany was a fourth-generation descendant of Georg Hermany, who emigrated from Hannover, Germany, to Berks County, Pennsylvania, in 1765. After experiments by George Warren Fuller in the late 1890s, Hermany designed the Crescent Hill treatment plant. The Louisville Water Company began to deliver filtered water in 1909, reducing typhoid deaths from seventy-one per thousand to less than forty-five. Beginning in 1914, chlorine was added to the water.

The Louisville Water Tower located east of downtown Louisville is the oldest ornamental water tower in the world. The water tower and its pumping station are on the National Register of Historic Places. As with the Fairmount Water Works of Philadelphia (designed in 1812 and completed in 1822), the industrial nature of the Louisville Water Tower was disguised in the form of a Greek temple complex.

A tornado on March 27, 1890, severely damaged the water tower. The original water tower had an iron pipe protected by a wood-paneled shaft, but after the tornado destroyed it, it was replaced with cast iron. The tornado also destroyed all but two of the ten statues that adorned the pedestals. Shortly thereafter, a new pumping station and reservoirs were built in Crescent Hill, and the original water tower ceased pumping operations in 1909. The original pumping station was renovated in 2010, and in 2014 the Louisville Water Works Museum opened on its premises.

Chapter 8

TRADES

By Michael E. Maloney

S imply defined, a trade is a skilled job, typically requiring manual skills and special training, as compared to professional occupations such as teachers, doctors, lawyers, accountants, programmers and journalists. Of the more than fifty trades listed in the 1881 Louisville city directory, the surnames of the people involved in several trades are all German, such as musical instrument manufacturers and potters, while others show a significant German influence, including cabinet makers, where twelve of the fourteen listed were German or of German descent. Similarly, locksmiths showed eight of nine listings to be of German origin, while fifty-three of the sixty-eight listed tailors were of German descent. Of forty-eight milliners, thirty-three were women—sixteen with German surnames. The millinery trade, in particular, afforded young, unmarried women or widows an opportunity to provide for themselves.

When Johannes Bindner was born in 1833, his parents, Valentin and Maria Franzisca Geiger Bindner, of Steinfeld, Bavaria, could not have foretold the revolutionary events of 1848 that would shake the foundations of the various kingdoms that now form Germany. The young Bindner began his own journey across the ocean in 1856. He brought his most valued possession, his trade as a Korbmacher (basket maker). Settling in Louisville's Portland neighborhood in 1857, he married Magdelena Hasselback, also a Steinfeld native, and prospered in his occupation. His older brother Martin was a basket maker in Uptown, now known as the Phoenix Hill neighborhood.

Basket making represented an important skill—especially in the era before paper or plastic bags and cardboard boxes—and was one of many trades dominated by German immigrants and their offspring. In the 1880 Louisville directory, all eighteen of the listed basket makers had German surnames. Bindner joined this legion of immigrants, including fellow basket makers and brothers Adam and Anton Hauber. The Hauber brothers immigrated to America from Neupotz in the Rhineland-Palatinate in 1849 and settled in New Orleans before relocating to Portland, Kentucky, by 1852. Other family members, including their older brother, Wendel, who was also a basket maker, joined them in 1857.

A review of Louisville city directories, with verification of origin from online genealogy websites, provides the following sample of German immigrants engaged in Louisville trades:

Baden immigrant Franz C. Schubert worked as a collar maker along with his American-born sons Casper, August and Frank Jr.

Heinrich and Elizabeth Bender, natives of Gernsheim, Hessen-Darmstadt, immigrated in 1848 with their sons Conrad, a tinner, George, a barber and dentist, and Nicholas, also a barber. Nicholas died in the worst maritime disaster in United States history—the explosion of the dangerously overloaded steamer *Sultana*, following his release from a Confederate prison camp near the end of the Civil War.

Benedict Kraus, a carpenter, was born in 1869 in Louisville to carpenter Anton Kraus and his wife, Agatha Schmitt, who were natives of Rimmels, Hessen.

Erhart S. Weck, a chair caner, was born in Louisville in 1865 to immigrants Sylvester Weck and Catharina Hiermeier from Oberthal—near Bühlertal—Baden.

Brick maker and teamster Charles F. Vettiner was born in Hoffweier, Baden, in 1850 to Elizabeth Gegg and adopted by her husband, Johann George Vettiner, from Menzingen, Baden. He is the grandfather of the Charlie Vettiner Park's namesake.

Jacob Sauer, a master shoemaker, immigrated in 1857. He followed his older brother Gabriel, a tailor, who immigrated in 1848 and their cousin Louis. The whole family was from Sasbach am Kaiserstuhl, Baden.

Chair maker William Boemker was born in Hannover in 1831 and immigrated in 1850.

Butcher William Knop arrived in 1887 from Zwönitz, Prussia.

Sebastian Gruneisen was born in 1839 in Breisach, Baden. He was a Union States Army Civil War veteran who trained as a carpenter and later became a teamster in Louisville's thriving brewery industry.

Casper Feiock, a carpenter, was born in 1841 in Pittsburgh to Bavarian immigrants Ludwig and Caroline Feiock, who operated a brewery, saloons and a beer garden in New Albany. Feiock also held multiple co-patents relating to coopering.

Cooper John Fromang was born in 1845 in Ferdinand, Indiana, to Johann Fromang, an immigrant from Hommarting, Lorraine—an area of France steeped in Germanic culture—and his wife, Franziska Gramelspacher, from Bollschweil, Baden.

Exemplifying every aspect of *Deutschtum* (Germanness), these immigrants typify the many thousands of German settlers who established themselves in the Louisville region. They represented trades that were as tightly woven into German culture as beer and bratwurst: brewers, butchers, bakers, millers, photographers, jewelers, carriage and wagon makers, hatters, cigar makers, coopers, carpenters, electricians, plumbers, furniture makers, machinists, silversmiths, tanners, watch and clockmakers, milliners, tailors, undertakers, florists, masons and stonecutters. These trades showcased the talents of the German immigrants who enriched the Falls Cities of Louisville, Jeffersonville, Clarksville and New Albany.

Farmers, often referred to as gardeners in the nineteenth century, must also be considered. While they were not tradesmen, they sometimes operated trade-related businesses. For example, farmer Henry J. Kaiser (1836–1910), from Hessen-Darmstadt, worked with his sons, Henry, George, Charles and Conrad, as blacksmiths and wagon makers while also operating a tollhouse on the Bardstown Turnpike in the then New Hamburg area of Jefferson County, across from today's Bashford Manor. Additionally, machinist Martin A. Storch (1894–1972), later a policeman, was the son of Prussian immigrant and farmer Ferdinand J. Storch (1853–1929).

In the relatively new trade of photography, Louisville boasted fourteen studios in 1881. These were commonly called "galleries" because many of the shops featured additional artwork. Four of the best-known proprietors were immigrants from German-speaking nations. This included the Stuber brothers, Daniel (1833–1891) and Michael (1842–1884), from Steinwenden, Bavaria; Edward Klauber (1835–1918) from Bohemia; and J. Henry Doerr (1847–1906) from Grumbach, Bavaria.

The Stuber brothers immigrated to the United States with their parents in 1847. Daniel apprenticed as a saddler before turning to photography about 1853. He opened a studio about 1857 at Preston and Market Streets but moved to 434 East Market Street in 1864. Michael apprenticed as a photographer and had his own studio at Market and Jackson Streets until

Kaiser Blacksmith Shop. *Courtesy Wayne Hettinger.*

1877, when he and Daniel joined their businesses. Michael's Louisville-born son, William George Stuber (1864–1959), also an accomplished photographer, worked for the Stuber brothers' studio before relocating to Rochester, New York, where he eventually became the chairman and CEO of Eastman Kodak.

Edward Klauber immigrated to the United States in 1853 and moved to Louisville in 1855. He was a photographer for sixty years—first operating his Beehive Gallery on Main Street between Third and Fourth Streets, then Klauber's Gallery at Third and Jefferson Streets. Klauber developed a national reputation for his photographs of prominent theatrical personalities and for his documentary works.

J. Henry Doerr immigrated to the United States with his parents in 1852. He started as an apprentice for Edward Klauber at age fourteen, but after a short time, he started his own photography business. His final studio location, where he worked for twenty-seven years, was at Twelfth and Market Streets.

Typical of many families whose sons practiced the same trade as their father, Christian Ullrich Jr., born in 1849 in Altengronau, Hessen, was the oldest of four sons of shoemaker Christian Ullrich Sr., who shared

Edward Klauber photograph of U.S. Lifesaving Service members at the Grand Industrial Parade, 1882. *Left to right*: Charles Fuller, John Gillooly, George Trager, William Smith, Captain William Devan, John Martin, Ed Farrell, Joseph Martin and William Drazel. *Courtesy Mary Catherine Farrell Beck, Janice Beck Ising and Sharon Beck Hartman.*

his trade with each of his sons. Altengronau, a small village of only about one thousand inhabitants, presented limited opportunities to so many shoemakers. Aided by sponsorship from Louisville's St. Luke Evangelical Church, brothers Christian and Johann Adam immigrated to the United States in 1881. Christian continued shoemaking from his shop and home at 1728 West Main Street until his death in 1916, while Adam practiced baking for most of his career. The Ullrich home in Altengronau is known as "Das Schusterhaus" and retains the Ullrich surname on its façade.

Jacob N. Pfeiffer (1861–1925), a hatter and merchant tailor, succeeded Manuel Rosenfield (1840–1928) in 1883 at his Seventh and Market Streets shop, which opened in 1870. Pfeiffer was born in Louisville to Jacob, a Prussian immigrant and cooper, and Baden native Barbara Staible Pfeiffer. He married Elizabeth Frickhoeffer (1860–1929) in 1884 and was joined in business by Hessen-Darmstadt immigrant and tailor Philipp C. Klapper (1853–1901), who arrived in New Orleans but moved to Louisville before 1878. Klapper married Maria Wilhelmina Frickhoeffer (1854–1928), Elizabeth's sister. Elizabeth and Maria were daughters of Carl (1829–1899), a tailor, and Henrietta Deusser Frickhoeffer (1833–1896), immigrants from Burgschwalbach, Prussia.

Right: Cast-iron shoe forms once owned by Johann Adam Ullrich. *Courtesy David Nichols.*

Below: Jacob N. Pfeiffer and Company, Hatters and Merchant Tailors, about 1900. *Courtesy J. William and Katherine H. Klapper.*

Alsatian Philip Sengel (1854–1937), a master cooper, emigrated from Brumath, Alsace, in 1872 following the Franco-Prussian War. He founded Gambrinus Cooperage Works, which specialized in all types of barrels to store beers, wines, bourbon and foodstuffs, in 1880. Sengel named his company for Gambrinus, the legendary German folk hero of brewers, who is also celebrated in the "Gambrinus March," a song composed for the Louisville Gambrinus Society in 1898, with score by Constanin Kollros (1838–1916) and lyrics by Frank A. Lenz. In 1893 the cooperage received the highest award for its products at Chicago's Columbian Exposition. Crippled by Prohibition in 1920, the enterprise aggressively went public after repeal in 1933, when only one million wooden kegs remained—down from a pre–Eighteenth Amendment high of seventeen million. Sengel died due to complications from injuries suffered while evacuating his Logan Street home during the 1937 flood. His son George (1888–1971) succeeded him in business, but with the introduction of metal kegs in the late 1950s, demand for Gambrinus products fell.

In 1880 Prussian immigrant Elizabeth Lang Pfiester (1837–1912), a forty-two-year-old widow, continued her Bavarian-native husband Peter's (1833–1879) thriving cooperage along with their son George (1860–1946). Elizabeth and Peter's daughter Elizabeth Pfiester (1858–1940) married Theodore Ahrens (1859–1938), a benefactor of Ahrens Trade School. Their other daughter Caroline (1862–1957) married Theodore Tafel (1848–1952), a Henryville, Indiana–born surgical instrument manufacturer and son of Stuttgart natives Carl (1825–1897) and Pauline Autenreith Tafel (1832–1913). They are ancestors of Mercedes-Benz of Louisville founder John Andrews Tafel, who died in 2018.

In the 1870s, tradesmen began to formalize their occupations by forming associations, or unions, rooted in the traditions of ancient European guilds. As noted by John Hennen in a *Kentucky Historical Register* article,

> *After the Civil War, the United States was transformed by urbanization and large-scale industrialization. Within Kentucky that transformation was originally concentrated in Louisville, Newport, and Covington… composed of a diverse working class of European immigrants, liberated blacks, and internal migrants….The Knights of Labor had 177 local assemblies in Kentucky in 1886, mostly in Louisville and Covington, at the peak of its national prominence.*

Many immigrant tradesmen or their descendants played key roles in these early movements. Labor leader Fred W. Schwenker (1850–1917), who arrived in the United States from Nordholz, Hannover, in 1871, was pivotal in organizing the bartending trade in 1897, became editor and publisher of the *Journal of Labor* in 1905 and served on the Louisville Board of Aldermen from 1911 until his death, when flags in the city were ordered

Gambrinus Cooperage Works letterhead, 1902. *Courtesy C. Robert and Victoria A. Ullrich.*

to fly at half-staff, and Mayor John H. Buschemeyer (1869–1935) served as a pallbearer.

Son of the aforementioned John Fromang, Frank R. Fromang (1886–1917), a butcher, worked closely with Pat Gorman (1892–1980), later a nationally prominent labor leader, to help build one of the early meatpacking unions before his untimely death at age thirty-one.

Many assemblies of tradesmen, when not meeting in Liederkranz Hall, Beck's Hall, the Union Labor Temple on Market Street or other locales, met at Louisville's popular Phoenix Hill Park. Frank Fromang's daughter Elinor Fromang Maloney (1913–2002) wrote years later,

> *I also had some fancy union badges and souvenirs from the annual Labor Day picnic at Phoenix Hill Park on Baxter Avenue. My father loved these gatherings with the speeches, the wheels, and the bratwurst. Mother and father walked from their home on Mellwood Avenue across the Morning Star Bridge to Baxter Avenue. They carried me and showed me off to the lodge folks. I barely remember this as a blur of music, people and food.*

Most of these tradesmen did not make the headlines, nor did they have streets named for them, but they did typeset those same headlines and build those same streets—an incalculable addition to the growth of Louisville and its surrounding communities. Their descendants still contribute to our region. This rich legacy produced hundreds of businesses, including several notable companies and institutions—current and past—featured in the following paragraphs:

Bosse Funeral Home: Bosse Funeral Home was founded in 1865 by Henry Bosse (1838–1908) from Bad Iburg, Hannover, who arrived in

Louisville in 1853. Bosse's cabinetmaking trade led to a U.S. government contract to build coffins during the Civil War. Bosse was joined by his brother Joseph (1840–1913), also a cabinetmaker, who immigrated in 1860. Another brother and farmer, Bernard (1846–1924), immigrated in 1872 with their mother, Maria Gertrude Vornholt Bosse (1808–1881), his wife, Catherine Heheman Bosse (1846–1909), and their infant son, Franz "Frank" Henry (1871–1971). Bernard first worked in the machinist and teamster trades before joining the funeral home firm in about 1878 as a driver and later a stable master. Henry Bosse's grandson, Robert G. Bosse (1896–1979), cofounded both Embry-Bosse Funeral Home on Preston Street in 1950 and Highlands Funeral Home on Taylorsville Road in 1960. Bosse Funeral Home, located at Barrett and Ellison Avenues since 1951, still operates under fourth-generation Bosse descendants— members of the William H. Wagner (1925–2013) family. Additional partners include W. Ray Flamm, J. Robert Reed (1939–2017)—the well-known Germantown and Schnitzelburg fixture—his wife, Lynda Boehnlein Reed, their son, G. Anthony Reed, and his wife, Carol, as well as Paul Moon.

Buschemeyer's Jewelers: Hannover immigrants William Buschemeyer, a baker, his wife, Helena, and their five children settled in Jeffersonville, Indiana, in 1864. Their son, William G. Buschemeyer (1861–1943), founded Buschemeyer's Jewelers, which traces its roots to 1865 as the successor to August Rees (1845–1887), a silversmith and manufacturing jeweler from Genheim amt Ettenheim, Baden. Buschemeyer and Charles E. Seng bought Rees's business in April 1887, just two weeks before Rees's unanticipated death, and operated as Buschemeyer and Seng until 1896. Buschemeyer's Jewelers became the first tenant in the Starks Building when it opened in 1914. Having lost both wife Fannie and son William

William G. Buschemeyer.
Courtesy University of Louisville Rare Books.

in 1923, surviving daughters sold the business in 1944 to Harry Lawson, who died just three months later in February 1945. In 1949, James D. Davis (1918–2014) acquired the firm from the Buschemeyer estate and operated it with his son, Leslie, before the final Douglass Loop store closed in 2017.

Dolfinger's: Jacob Dolfinger (1820–92) immigrated in 1847 and founded his company about 1851. Born in Weil der Stadt, Württemberg, Dolfinger, a gold- and silversmith, began to specialize in imported fine china, crystal and glassware by 1863. His partners were his sons, Otto (1845–1918) and Edward (1852–1933), and Bavarian immigrant George Zoeller (1833–1889), who was a noted musician. Otto retired from business in 1894, leaving Edward to manage the company until closing in May 1926 and relocating with his wife to New York to live with daughter, Emma (1881–1927), a prominent figure in the American Child Health Association. Following Emma's unexpected death in January 1927, Dolfinger returned to Louisville, reopened his business in 1928 and retired again in 1932. Once totaling eight stores, Dolfinger's now operates in St. Matthews and at the Galt House.

J. Edinger and Son: A fourth-generation company founded in 1867 by Jacob Edinger (1837–1913), this East Main Street business remains a staple in the Butchertown neighborhood. Edinger, Pennsylvania-born son of immigrants John George and Rosina Schneider Edinger, trained as a blacksmith. The company originally produced horse-drawn carriages and wagons before transitioning to the automotive market.

Jacob Edinger Wagon Manufacturing Company. *Courtesy University of Louisville Photographic Archives.*

Heimerdinger's Cutlery Company: August Heimerdinger (1831–1888) from Göppingen, Württemberg, founded this now fifth-generation family business in 1861, operating downtown before relocating to St. Matthews in 1983. Originally manufacturing scissors and knives, August's son, William C. (1862–1917), and grandson, William G. (1894–1981), both held patents for knives, shears and razors. In 1947 his great-grandson, Henry W. (born 1926), entered the business, working closely with his wife, Betty, until his retirement in 1991. Manufacturing continued until the mid-1950s, and a hardware division continued until the mid-1960s. Today, Heimerdinger's carries a full line of cutlery, shears, scissors and barber supplies and is operated by August's great-great-grandson, Carl Heimerdinger, and his wife, Glenna Fahle.

Marcus Paint Company: Marcus Paint Company was founded in 1853 by Prussian immigrant Herman Marcus (1823–1908), who was a master painter. The company, located on East Market Street for more than one hundred years, is one of America's oldest continually operating paint manufacturers.

Nanz and Kraft Florists: Nanz and Kraft was founded by Stuttgart-born Henry Nanz Sr. (1821–91) in 1850. Nanz Sr. landed in New Orleans in 1847 and, following a stint in Texas, headed north with a column of soldiers returning from Mexico. He reached Jeffersonville, Indiana, in 1848. A trained horticulturist, he found employment with the celebrated Colonel Robert Johnson Ward family—father of the famous Sallie Ward (1827–1896)—showcasing his trade to the delight of his many wealthy friends. Nanz's first nursery stood on an acre of land on Third Street between Breckinridge and Kentucky Streets. Known as Nanz, Neuner and Company in 1872, when Henry Nanz Jr. (1857–1923) and future son-in-law and Württemberg native Carl Neuner (1848–1900), joined the business, Nanz Sr. purchased thirty acres of land at Gilman's Point (now St. Matthews) about 1874. His daughter, Sallie Ward Nanz (1850–1913), married Prussian native and wholesale butcher Henry A. Kraft Jr. (1839–1915) in 1869. Sallie and Henry's grandson, Edward August Kraft Jr. (1907–67), assumed ownership of the florist shop in 1958. The business later passed to next-generation descendant Edward Ramsey Kraft (born 1938) and today is operated by sons Edward and David Kraft, who had worked with their brother Michael until his death in 2019.

Ratterman Funeral Homes: The Ratterman family—parents Gerhard, a farmer, and Maria, as well as two siblings—traveled from Ankum, Hannover, to Cincinnati in 1845. Ratterman brothers George

(1836–1889), a carpenter, and Herman (1839–1883), a cabinetmaker, relocated to Louisville and opened their shop in 1864, listing it in 1866 as "G. & H. Ratterman, furniture dealers and undertakers." George's son, John B. Ratterman (1878–1949), married brewing magnate Philip Ackerman's (1841–1914) daughter Lillian (1880–1962) in 1904. The couple had twelve children—ten boys and two girls—and lived and worked from the Ackerman home at 2114 West Market Street beginning in 1914. The Lexington Road home opened in 1939, operated by sons John Jr. (1911–94) and Carl Sr. (1914–2003). In 1947 Joseph Sr. (1921–1997) and Cletus (1920–2015) opened the Fourth Street home, expanding in 1977 to Southside Drive. In 1963 Emmett Sr. (1918–2011) and Oscar (1909–1988) followed on Bardstown Road, expanding to Cane Run Road in 1974. All of these funeral homes are now operated by the fourth and fifth generations of the Ratterman family as four separate businesses.

Julius Schnurr and Sons: Immigrating in 1890 from Obersasbach, Baden, mason and plasterer Julius Schnurr (1871–1947), joined by brothers Gustav (1873–1947) and Stephan (1876–1961), also plasterers, founded a business in 1892 that thrives to this day. Julius Schnurr and Sons notably renovated Louisville Metro Hall's exterior in 2017. The business is now operated by fourth-generation descendants from 820 Logan Street—the former home of Gambrinus Cooperage's Philip Sengel.

Seng Jewelers: Charles E. Seng (1864–1940), following the dissolution of his partnership with William G. Buschemeyer, opened a jewelry store in 1891 according to period advertisements, though contemporary information suggests it opened in 1889. Seng's brother Louis (1862–1935) also operated a jewelry store and had worked for August Rees in the early 1880s. The Seng brothers were born in Louisville to Bavarian immigrant Heinrich Seng (1806–83) and his wife, Elizabeth Zinct Seng (1824–89), from Kurhessen. Benn B. Davis (1915–2014) purchased the business in 1938, which is now managed by his son Lee and grandson Scott. Seng moved to the Starks Building on South Fourth Street in 1983, then to One Riverfront Plaza in 2019. Buschemeyer's Jimmy Davis and Seng's Benn Davis were brothers.

Chapter 9

MEDICINE

By Katherine Burger Johnson

I t is widely accepted that the first German-born immigrant to arrive in Louisville was A.D. Ehrich, a shoemaker, who came in 1817. At this time, there was a total of twenty-four doctors to serve the medical needs of the four thousand residents of Louisville. This was a time when a doctor was only called as a last resort and it appeared death was imminent. With fewer than a dozen medical schools in the country, many of these practitioners were self-trained or had studied with a practicing physician until ready to "hang out a shingle."

In his 1873 history of the "German Element" in Louisville, Ludwig Stierlin wrote that the first three physicians of German birth to arrive in Louisville were Doctors Lauth, Kafka and Holland. A Doctor Donhoff (most likely Albert von Donhoff, born in 1806 in Berlin, died in 1882 in Louisville) arrived soon thereafter. A lengthy article in the *Courier-Journal* on November 10, 1889, contained extensive coverage of many local German individuals, organizations and topics, but the only mention of these doctors was their names, thus illustrating the low status of medical practitioners at this time. Receiving much more coverage were German-language newspapers, music societies and concerts, churches and businesses.

Due to variations in spelling, it is often difficult to determine when and where certain doctors were living and practicing. The list of physicians in the 1838–39 city directory includes William J.C. Baum, Doctor Calphka (possibly Kafka), Richard Wantyn and John Gerber. Five years later, Baum, Kafka and Wantyn were listed, as well as Martin Anzi, William

Bodenhamer and Donhoff. The names of these doctors appear in the 1840 census of Louisville, along with several others who may have been German immigrants: Doctors William Casper, Kohler, Winter, H. Preissler and Richard Wanton (possibly Wantyn). The 1832 city directory, the first published in Louisville, does not list any physicians with German surnames.

Life was not easy for some of these men. Doctor Donhoff (possibly von Donhoff) was reported to have only one patient in his first year of practice, and that patient did not pay his fee. His practice must have increased at some point, as he continued to be listed in the city directories for more than thirty-two years. It is said that in 1844 Doctor Holland, who opposed slavery, had to hide in Indiana as a gang from Kentucky searched for him. He managed to escape capture.

Another physician of German descent was Lewis D. Kastenbine, whose father immigrated to Louisville from Hannover in 1820. The doctor was born in 1839 and attended the University of Louisville Medical Department from 1860 to 1861 before serving as a medical cadet in the Civil War. He earned his medical degree from Bellevue in New York in 1864, then returned to Louisville to teach at three of the local medical schools.

Samuel D. Gross (1805–1884) is prominent in the history of medicine, especially the history of surgery. Born on a farm in Pennsylvania to Quakers of German descent, Gross grew up speaking no English. With the desire to become a physician, he read medicine with a local practitioner before attending and graduating from the Jefferson Medical College in Philadelphia in 1828. Before moving to Louisville in 1840 to chair the Department of Surgery at the Louisville Medical Institute (now the University of Louisville School of Medicine), he taught at two medical schools in Cincinnati. His writings on surgery and the treatment of wounds include *A System of Surgery* (1858) and *A Manual of Military Surgery* (1861). In 1867 he was elected president of the American Medical Association. In a 2010 article about Gross in the *Journal of the American College of Surgeons*, Neal Garrison and Lewis Flint concluded, "There is no suitable term to describe the contributions of Samuel David Gross to American surgery."

By 1851–52 there were 150 doctors listed in Louisville, including most of those named previously, with the addition of Lewis Cohn, John Hupfauf, Henry W. Koehler, John A. Krack, Ferdinand Krauth and John Lauth (possibly Laut).

Doctor John Hupfauf of Bavaria had trained in Tübingen and München (Munich) and was appointed physician to the Royal Bavarian Battalion in Würzburg in 1837. He joined the opposition forces during the German

Samuel David Gross statue, Philadelphia. *Courtesy Library of Congress.*

Revolution of 1848, escaped in 1849 and immigrated to Kentucky. He died in Louisville in 1863 and had a son who fought for the Union and was killed in May 1864 at the Battle of Pickett's Mill in Georgia.

Another doctor who came as a Forty-Eighter was Charles A. Fischer. Born in Saxony in about 1820, he arrived in the United States in 1850. In February 1862 he enlisted in the 32nd Regiment of the Indiana Volunteer Infantry as a chaplain but served mainly as a surgeon. He was discharged due to a disability in October of that year and died in 1867 from dysentery contracted during his wartime service.

John Augustus Krack was born in 1823 in Baltimore to a Lutheran pastor and his wife, who then moved to Indiana. Krack taught school in Henry County, Kentucky, before moving to Louisville to study medicine under the renowned Joshua Flint. He took one course of studies at the Kentucky School of Medicine and graduated in the first class of the new school in 1851. He began his practice of medicine but soon became a businessman and a politician. He owned pharmacies and a glass company, served on the school board, the city's Common Council and Board of Aldermen and worked as city assessor.

Chaplain Charles A. Fischer, 32nd
Regiment, Indiana Volunteer Infantry.
Courtesy Library of Congress.

The Wathen family also settled in Kentucky prior to the 1848 influx, arriving in Nelson County in 1787. William H. Wathen attended St. Mary's College near Lebanon and then the University of Louisville Medical Department, where he graduated in 1870. He practiced in Louisville, taught gynecological and abdominal surgery at the Kentucky School of Medicine and served as dean for fifteen years.

Probably the most prominent Louisville medical family of German descent is the Flexner family, which made great contributions to health care and medical education. The father, Moritz (1819–92), emigrated from Bavaria, making his way to Louisville via Strasbourg, France, New York and New Orleans. He met and married Esther Abraham (1834–1905), originally from the Rhineland-Palatinate near the French border, in 1855. They had seven sons and two daughters. Two of their sons studied medicine and one conducted the most comprehensive survey of medical education to date in this country.

Jacob, the oldest of the Flexner children, postponed his medical studies when the family suffered a financial setback. He attended pharmacy school in 1878 and began working to pay for his brothers' education. In later years, he was able to go to medical school himself at the Louisville Medical College, graduating in 1902.

His younger brother Simon Flexner worked with Jacob at the pharmacy and attended the Louisville College of Pharmacy, graduating in 1882. He then went on to the Louisville Medical College, graduating in 1899 and followed that with studies at Johns Hopkins University, as well as in Prague and Strasbourg. He had an illustrious research career, serving on the faculty of Johns Hopkins University, 1892–98; the University of Pennsylvania, 1899–1903; and as director of the Rockefeller Institute of Medical Research, 1903–35. In 1899 he isolated a strain of dysentery

Abraham Flexner. *Courtesy University of Louisville Photographic Archives.*

bacillus and used it to develop a cure for cerebrospinal meningitis. He also trapped the polio virus for laboratory study, work that was continued by Albert Sabin and resulted in the oral polio vaccine.

The third Flexner brother in medicine, Abraham, is considered among the one hundred most important Americans of the twentieth century. Not a physician, he became an educator and is recognized for his groundbreaking research on medical education published in 1910. In this, Flexner reported that American medical schools should adopt the German model of studies and clinical experience. His influence is still felt in the twenty-first century, with historians and physicians studying and using his work to improve medical education. A street in the Louisville Medical Center is named for him.

The interest in medicine carried on to the next generation of Flexners. Louis B. Flexner (1902–1996), son of the youngest brother, Washington, fulfilled his dream of a medical career with the financial assistance of his uncles Simon and Abraham. He went on to chair the Department of Anatomy at the University of Pennsylvania School of Medicine and was well-known for his research in the biochemistry of memory.

One particular Louisville family with well-known legal connections also has a long medical tradition. Samuel Brandeis (1819–1889), an uncle of Supreme Court justice Louis D. Brandeis, was a respected Louisville physician. The family came from Prague, where Samuel received his formative education. He then studied medicine in Vienna, graduating in 1845. The family left their native land in 1849 due to political unrest and originally settled in Madison, Indiana. In 1852 they moved to Louisville, where Samuel built a thriving practice. He is credited with introducing the hypodermic syringe and the laryngoscope to Kentucky. He and his wife, Caroline, who was also from Prague, had seven children. At least two of their children became physicians, including their daughter Florence Brandeis (1860–1941), who graduated from the Women's Medical College of Pennsylvania in 1894. She followed this with additional study in Europe before returning to Louisville to practice in 1896.

Carl Weidner Sr. (1857–1943) was a pioneer in the use of the microscope for medical research. He was born in Hessen-Kassel and grew up interested in the natural sciences. He worked in apothecaries in Germany and then in the United States after immigrating and while attending the Kentucky School of Medicine, from which he graduated in 1881. On a trip to Germany, he learned about the use of the microscope and introduced the study of bacteriology to medical students in Louisville.

Louis Kaelin. *Courtesy Irma Kaelin Raque.*

Louis (Alois) Kaelin (1857–1919) was born in Euthal, near Einsiedeln, Switzerland. Upon completing medical studies at the University of Berlin in 1884, he immigrated to Louisville, where he became a well-known and highly respected general practitioner. In 1893 he married Mary Elizabeth Striegel, and they had four children. He was a member of many local Swiss organizations, and from 1887 until his death, he served as the consul of the Swiss Confederation for Kentucky.

One of the earliest female physicians in Louisville came from Germany. Little is known about Marie (Maria) Gutterman Graff Scott, other than that she was born about 1840 and immigrated to the United States in 1872. One source lists her birth name as Rothenmeier, and an Amsterdam population index shows her living there and leaving in May 1862. It is not clear if Gutterman or Graff are earlier married names, but in 1910 James E. Scott is listed as her husband. She is buried in Cave Hill Cemetery.

Another important German addition to the Louisville medical community was Lotte Bernstein (1896–1971), a psychiatrist trained at the University of Berlin (graduated 1924). Bernstein fled Germany in 1935, then lived in Norway and Sweden before immigrating to the United States in 1951. She served as clinical director of what became the Child Guidance Clinic and was innovative in her support of using art and music in psychotherapy.

Germans also established several hospitals in Louisville. These included the German Methodist Deaconess Hospital (1895–1951); the Methodist Evangelical Hospital, founded in 1960 by Louisville's German Methodist and Evangelical churches; St. Anthony Hospital, founded in 1902 by an order of Franciscan nuns from Westphalia; and Jewish Hospital, incorporated in 1903 and dedicated in 1905. These institutions played a vital role in making Louisville a medical center in the twentieth century. A list of the early medical staff at Jewish Hospital reads like a veritable German "Who's Who" of local physicians, including I.A. Lederman, J.A. Flexner, F.W. Fleischaker, Leon L. Solomon, Siegal C. Frankel, Sidney H. Meyers, DeWitt Henry H. Wolfe, Florence Brandeis, Leo Bloch, I.N. Bloom, Herbert Bronner, Lee Kahn and Oscar E. Bloch.

A more contemporary medical practice with a worldwide reputation is the Kleinert, Kutz and Associates Hand Care Center established by Harold E. Kleinert (1921–2013) in 1953. Joseph Kutz joined the practice in 1964, and it grew to be the largest practice of hand specialists in the world, seeing thousands of patients and training more than twelve hundred physicians from fifty-eight countries.

The influence of German culture and education continues to this day. Young physicians from Germany have come to Louisville to teach and practice. Miriam Krause, from Talheim, near Heilbronn, Baden-Württemberg, did three rotations at U.S. locations before graduating in 2006. After some time at Southern Illinois University, she went to the University of Louisville in 2011 for a fellowship in reproductive endocrinology and fertility.

Kathrin LaFaver earned her MD degree from Albert-Ludwigs Universität in 2005. After advanced training, she came to the United States for an internship at the Mayo Clinic in Rochester, Minnesota, followed by fellowships in Boston and Bethesda, Maryland. Since 2013 she has been with the division of movement disorders in the Department of Neurology at the University of Louisville School of Medicine.

Chapter 10

LEGAL ARTS

By Kevin Collins and Kathleen Pellegrino

In 1832 Louisville's population of ten thousand included forty attorneys. Today, about one in three Louisvillians claim German heritage. These two disparate observations suggest that (a) Louisville has always been litigiously well-prepared, and (b) German culture has provided a large number of legal practitioners whose full stories are impossible to recount. This chapter opts, with one exception, to trace generations of three significant German families that were exemplars of the legal profession during the period 1781 to 1989.

The brothers Isaac (1753–1794) and Abraham Hite Jr. (1754–1832) were residents of Jefferson County and the grandsons of Hans Jost Hite (1685–1761). Patriarch Hite, born in Württemberg, immigrated in 1709 as an "indentured Palatinate subsistence refugee." A linen weaver by trade, at his death Hans possessed the largest land holdings held by a private citizen in the Colony of Virginia. His grandsons would come to manifest these acquisitive abilities along with the accompanying necessary legal skills.

Kentucky, not a Commonwealth until 1792, was the frontier or backland of Virginia. In 1781 Isaac, originally sent as a surveyor, was appointed one of ten "Gentlemen Justices" on the first court ever convened in Kentucky. The duration of his service is unknown. He had no formal legal training, but his previous judicial experiences consisted of nine years intermittently serving as a justice of the peace in Colonial Virginia and later the Commonwealth of Virginia.

This first court in Kentucky met in Lincoln County. Administratively, it verified professional credentials, granted or accepted commissions (lawyers,

Isaac Hite House. *Courtesy Wikimedia Commons.*

surveyors, sheriffs, militia), regulated yearly prices (alcohol, grain, "warm or cold dinners," lodging), issued licenses for services, paid bills and levied fines (usually in tobacco). Judicially, wills, estates, land disputes, theft, gaming and alcohol were common cases.

Abraham Hite Jr. was a representative at the Kentucky Statehood Convention in Danville in 1788. In 1790 he was appointed one of five trustees of the town of Louisville. The incomplete *Jefferson County Kentucky Court Records, Volumes 1–4* indicate that he also sat as a "Gentleman Justice," probably from 1790 to 1796. This court acted as an examining court of undefined authority for white people, but for slaves it passed sentence, usually punishment by lash or hanging. Abraham also served as a senator in the Kentucky General Assembly from 1800 to 1803.

The extended Weissinger family provided five members to Louisville's legal history: George Washington Weissinger (1805–1850), George Weissinger Jr. (1836–1903), Rozel Weissinger (1848–1896), George Weissinger Smith (1864–1931) and Muir Weissinger (1870–1952). The family's American history began when Johann Georg Weissinger (1769–1837) emigrated from Stuttgart in Württemberg to Georgia in 1789. From there, he moved to Alabama.

Rozel Weissinger. *Courtesy Filson Historical Society.*

George Washington Weissinger, born in Georgia, moved to Louisville in 1828, having attended the Law Department of Transylvania University. He opened a law practice circa 1832. In 1835 he acquired half interest in the *Louisville Journal*. In his lifetime, he amassed considerable wealth and, through two marriages, contributed two sons and two grandsons to the legal profession.

Eldest son, George W. Weissinger Jr., graduated from Harvard in 1856 and the University of Louisville Law Department in 1858. After Confederate military service in which he lost an arm, Colonel Weissinger opened the law offices of Reid and Weissinger at 198 West Jefferson Street.

George's half-brother, Rozel, graduated from Princeton in 1868 and the University of Louisville Law Department in 1871. He subsequently served as its dean (1886–90) and professor of mercantile law and equity jurisprudence while maintaining a private law practice. He also served as a city councilman and state senator and authored a statute revising the law on injunctions.

Rozel was instrumental in the passage of the Weissinger Act, also called the Married Women's Property Act of 1894. Previously, Kentucky had functioned in concert with Blackstone's legal formulation stating, "By marriage, the husband and wife are one person in law: that is, the very being or legal existence of the woman is suspended during the marriage, or at least is incorporated and consolidated into that of the husband." Suffragists Josephine Henry and Laura Clay, among others, tired of being "suspended" and "incorporated," had campaigned long and hard for change. Rozel Weissinger shepherded the bill to law, securing married women's rights to make wills and, limitedly, to hold or dispose of property.

George Washington Weissinger's grandson George Weissinger Smith, a graduate of the University of Virginia in 1886 and the University of Louisville Law Department in 1887, practiced law with various Louisville partners for forty-four years. He served in the House of Representatives in 1898 and as Louisville's mayor from 1917 to 1921. He was elected on an anti-corruption and prohibition platform.

Another of George's grandsons, Muir Weissinger, a graduate of Columbia Law School in 1894, was elected as a Jefferson County judge (1910–13). He also served as judge on the Fiscal, Quarterly and Juvenile Courts, where he garnered a well-deserved reputation for his work with at-risk children, securing legislation for their placement in private homes instead of reform school.

The extended Wehle-Dembitz-Brandeis families, complexly intermarried, contributed at least seven members to the legal profession: Otto A. Wehle (1845–1931), Louis Brandeis Wehle (1880–1959), Lewis Naphtali Dembitz (1833–1907), Abraham Lincoln Dembitz (1867–1921), Nanette Dembitz (1912–1989), Supreme Court justice Louis Dembitz Brandeis (1856–1941) and Susan Brandeis Gilbert (1893–1975). These three families were not ancestrally German, but through traditions, education and native tongue, they were culturally German. Twenty-six members of these families left Prague in 1849, and by 1851 many of them had settled in Louisville.

Otto A. Wehle did not travel to the United States with the original families but arrived in 1867. He was twenty-two years old, had completed his studies in Vienna and was admitted to the Louisville bar on arrival. He practiced law in Louisville for more than fifty years. His various law partners included Lewis Dembitz, Louis Brandeis Wehle and Arthur M. Rutledge. He practiced corporate law, representing banks, tobacco companies and other concerns.

On December 17, 1921, the Louisville Bar Association established a Legal Aid Society to help "mothers and children…obtain sustenance from improvident fathers" and to aid the indigent accused of crime. Otto, whose obituary described him as a man of "broad human sympathies with a warm appreciation and kindness of heart," was a founding member.

Louis Brandeis Wehle, the second of Otto's four children, also practiced law in Louisville. He attended both Manual and Male High Schools, graduating in 1897. He earned his AB, MA and LLB degrees from Harvard, the latter in 1904. He practiced with his father until World War I, specializing in labor law and public works.

During the war, Louis provided legal services—negotiating contracts and arbitrating labor disputes—in areas of wartime production. He was general counsel for the War Finance Corporation, gaining expertise in foreign trade and international law. After 1921 he returned to private practice in New York and Washington, D.C. During and after World War II, Louis worked in England helping restore Europe's economy.

Lewis N. Dembitz, a child prodigy, was born in Zirke, Prussia, which is now part of Poland. He arrived in the United States at the age of sixteen

Lewis Naphtali Dembitz.
Courtesy University of Louisville Rare Books.

with the original group of émigrés from Prague. An autodidact with an Olympian command of a dozen languages—seven as a teenager—he moved to Louisville in 1851.

In 1852 he became a member of the bar. His previous legal education consisted of one semester studying Roman law at Charles University in Prague, followed by two years reading American law at the offices of Walker and Kilber, Cincinnati and one year with Dunn and Hendricks of Madison, Indiana. He practiced law in Louisville for more than fifty years. His partners included Martin Bijur (1860s), Otto Wehle (1870s) and his son, Abraham Lincoln Dembitz (1890s).

As assistant city attorney in 1884, Lewis Dembitz created a new tax collection system for Louisville. In 1888 he drafted the secret ballot law for the protection of Louisville voters—reputedly the first in American law. He was an expert in land dispute cases, authoring *Land Titles in the United States* (1895). He also authored *Kentucky Jurisprudence* (1890), among other books. He had a scholar's command of Jewish theology and customs, astronomy and higher mathematics, and he exercised a worldwide correspondence in pursuit of his intellectual interests.

This immense knowledge, housed in a diminutive frame of five feet and one hundred pounds, came with a playful sense of humor. Judge Bland Ballard, hearing a case in which he seemed to favor the Dembitz argument, but wishing to consider it overnight, ruled adversely the next morning. The judge confessed that he had engaged in overnight consultation with his wife, whereupon Dembitz, replied, "The next time I have a case in this court, I hope I may have the privilege of a hearing before the full bench."

Lewis's son, Abraham Lincoln Dembitz, an 1887 graduate of the University of Louisville Law Department, practiced with his father for about twelve years before moving to Washington, D.C. Abraham's daughter, Nanette, a 1938 graduate of Columbia Law School, served with distinction for fifteen years on the Bench of Family Court in New York.

United States Supreme Court justice Louis Dembitz Brandeis is one of the most esteemed figures in American and international law. Books chronicling his life, thought and influence number almost eight hundred, some fifty in foreign languages.

Born in Louisville in 1856, Brandeis was the son of two of the original Prague émigrés and was named after his uncle Lewis Dembitz. He attended English and German schools in Louisville and abroad. He graduated from Male High School in 1872, winning a gold medal "for pre-eminence in all his studies." In 1875 he was accepted to Harvard

Louis Dembitz Brandeis. *Courtesy Library of Congress.*

Law School by special waiver without an undergraduate degree. He excelled there, graduating in 1877. In 1887 he became one of the founders of the *Harvard Law Review* and later was the first justice to cite a law review in an opinion.

Brandeis was a practicing attorney for almost forty years, earning public approbation as "the people's attorney" for his work, *pro bono publico*, protecting the rights of the general public from corporate monopolies, establishing the constitutionality of many state statutes for maximum hour and minimum wage conditions, arbitrating labor disputes and instituting savings bank insurance policies. Today, many of these victories are commonly accepted practice.

In 1890 the *Harvard Law Review* published "The Right to Privacy" by Brandeis and his law partner, Samuel Warren. One of the most cited law review articles ever, it led the way to what Brandeis later called "the most comprehensive of rights, and the right most valued by civilized man." This is the right to be left alone. Brandeis's future judicial decisions would expand and clarify this insight.

Muller v. Oregon (1908) concerned maximum hours for women working in laundries. It was the first use of the "Brandeis Brief," employing expert testimony from other disciplines and emphasizing the facts to which the law applied. It introduced a new dimension to legal thought and is now the model for constitutional cases such as the momentous civil rights case *Brown v. Board of Education of Topeka*.

President Woodrow Wilson appointed Brandeis to the Supreme Court. The first Jew so appointed, and a known ardent progressive, his confirmation vote of 47–22 was contentious. He served for twenty-two years, during which he developed the modern jurisprudence of free speech (*Gilbert v. Minnesota*, 1920; *Gitlow v. New York*, 1925; *Whitney v. California*, 1927) and the constitutionally protected right to privacy (*Olmstead v. United States*, 1928). Of his seventy-four dissenting opinions, the Supreme Court eventually adopted most as correct constitutional constructs.

Brandeis never forgot his Louisville roots. He began donating books, papers and money to the University of Louisville about 1924 and continued this over his lifetime, arranging for the school to be one of only thirteen Supreme Court repositories. He eschewed foundation and corporate donations in favor of local participation, believing that the university would thrive only by fostering local loyalties and support. He said, "It is essentially Kentuckian, an institution for Kentuckians developed by Kentuckians." In 1998 the University's Law School was renamed in honor of Brandeis, and his and his wife's ashes repose beneath its portico.

Brandeis's daughter, Susan Brandeis Gilbert, also embraced the legal profession, graduating from the University of Chicago Law School in 1919. In 1925 she appeared before the Supreme Court regarding the War Insurance Act, necessitating her father's recusal. Her client lost.

In a story published June 6, 1914, with the headline, "Three Young Women Now Full-Fledged Lawyers," the *Courier-Journal* announced that for the first time in the history of the Law Department at the University of Louisville, three members of an eleven-person graduating class were women. Laura Lee Wehner (1887–1945) graduated with first honors and won the senior prize.

Wehner, whose grandparents emigrated from Hessen, was the daughter of Valentine Wehner, a boilermaker, and Mary L. Heidenrich Wehner. Following graduation, she attended Spencerian Commercial School and, according to the city directory, worked until 1920 as a law secretary at the welding business run by her brother Bernard.

By November 1920, a *Courier-Journal* story headlined "Louisville Women Invade Men's Field" noted several additional women attending law school but identified Laura Lee as the only then-practicing woman lawyer in the city. "Future husbands will gladly contribute the legal allowance to the wife

Laura Lee Wehner. *Courtesy Louisville Bar Association.*

when the mother comes marching home with a volume of the statutes under her arm," Miss Wehner told the newspaper. "My clients are about equally divided, and I warn the lawyers to guard well their positions, for woman is about to begin an unprecedented study of a science until recently known only to the trousered few."

On November 20, 1921, in a trial that was reported to be "the first time a woman conducted a case in court unaided," she won a verdict of $106.39 for the Rapler Sugar Feed Company. The judgment represented the full amount sought in the suit.

She was for several years the only practicing female lawyer in the city and was the first to try a case before a jury, according to the *Who's Who in Louisville* of 1926. Starting in 1933, she practiced in the Louisville City Attorney's Office. She chaired the Committee on the Legal Status of Women for the Louisville League of Women Voters. She was also a member of the Louisville Bar Association, where her photograph hangs on the wall among the other members of the class of 1925.

Chapter 11

FINE ARTS

By David P. Taylor

In the nineteenth century, Louisville and the Falls of the Ohio opened their arms to immigrants from all across Europe. Those arriving from Germany identified immediately with the landscape on either side of the Ohio River, finding the area's topography and native species remarkably similar to their fatherland. Encouraged by the opportunities of a progressive city and comforted by their geographical surroundings, men, women and families made an immediate and life-changing decision: Louisville would become their home. With confidence, determination and visions of better lives, they began anew.

Reports of Louisville's growing German community, the individual successes and the seemingly unlimited opportunities reached across the Atlantic and ushered wave after wave of newcomers. The nineteenth century saw the arrival of four individuals who, in time, would significantly transform Louisville's art scene. All German-born, three arrived as children, their talents already identified by accomplished European artists and instructors. The fourth arrived in New Orleans and settled in Alabama. He would later relocate to Louisville and establish a portrait studio that would span four decades. Some of the child artists had been accepted to prestigious art academies. One, at the age of nine, had participated competitively and won top honors. Another's talents, yet to be identified, would place him at the right hand of one of America's wealthiest publishers.

Artistic careers are composed of unending efforts, evolving styles and countless setbacks. Days are torn between the passion to create and the necessity of providing life's basic needs. For most, monetary gains were minimal. Parental skepticism and concern for their children's futures was warranted. One father opposed his son's artistic aspirations with cruel and heartbreaking behavior. Francis Bacon once wrote, "If the affection or aptness of the children be extraordinary, then it's good not to cross it." Undaunted, this particular youngster followed his artistic calling. Of the four careers presented, one spanned nearly a century. Another was cut short in the stride of his career. Their art and legacies have now extended far beyond the confines of metropolitan Louisville and the state of Kentucky.

NICOLA MARSCHALL

Nicola Marschall (1829–1917), born in Sankt Wendel in the Saarland, was an artistically gifted child. When he was barely a teen, he was already a serious student in various German ateliers. Success came early. He later wrote of himself, "I could draw or paint a fairly recognizable likeness when I was six or seven years old, and I knew how to criticize a picture almost that soon."

A three-month passage across the Atlantic at age twenty brought him to the Port of New Orleans. By 1873 he had migrated to Louisville with a significant résumé. He had established his own portrait studio and become an instructor of art, languages, music and dance at the Marion (Alabama) Female Seminary. Returning to Europe, he studied in Rome, Florence, Paris, Düsseldorf and Munich. When he returned to the United States, he went to Alabama.

With war on the horizon, he was approached about creating the Confederate flag. His design, the Stars and Bars, was raised in Montgomery on March 4, 1861. He also was responsible for the Confederacy's gray uniform. While serving four years in the Confederate States army, he was a draftsman and advisor to Robert E. Lee. His Marion portrait studio flourished. He painted the likenesses of countless southern families and dignitaries in addition to Confederate notables, such as Jefferson Davis, John C. Breckinridge and Nathan Bedford Forrest. Itinerant work became a necessity due to postwar conditions in the ravaged South. These conditions prompted him to move his family to Louisville.

Upon arrival in 1873, he immediately opened a studio at Fourth and Green (Liberty) Streets that would span forty years. After his passing in 1917,

Portrait of Jenny and Preston Green by Nicola Marschall. *Courtesy David P. and Marilyn Taylor.*

the studio inventory reportedly contained portraits of every United States president from Abraham Lincoln to Theodore Roosevelt. Nicola Marschall, recognized as "The Artist of the Confederacy," is buried in Louisville's Cave Hill Cemetery, where a state historical marker recognizes his gravesite and lifetime of artistic accomplishment.

CARL CHRISTIAN BRENNER

Carl Christian Brenner (1838–1888), born in Lauterecken, Bavaria, was Louisville's most accomplished German-born landscape artist. He attended public schools from ages six through fourteen, and this is where his talents were recognized. A teacher requested from King Ludwig I that Brenner be admitted to the Academy of Fine Arts in Munich. His father refused consent and trained his son as a glazier.

The family immigrated to the United States in 1853 by way of New Orleans but moved to Louisville during the winter of 1853–54. Rather than with a brush, his first artistic effort involved an attempt at carving. Little knife

93

in hand, he searched for the perfect piece of wood. Quietly, he removed himself to a corner and began to whittle. With admiration, he soon finished a perfect little plough, took it to his father and placed it in his hand. The latter received it, gazed upon it for a moment, then deliberately threw it on the floor and crushed it with his foot. This triumphant rebuke to his son's artistic endeavors not only proved unsuccessful but further magnified the boy's determination.

The brush replaced the knife, and his first painting was a miniature of a young general riding into battle, sword raised, brass buttons shining, mounted upon a billy goat. At the outset of the Civil War, Carl was twenty-three, just old enough to enter the service. He was assigned as a drummer for the Union forces. The war's conclusion brought him home, and he became a sign painter. His leisure time was spent covering canvases, focusing primarily on landscapes. Mr. Lindsay, owner of a Louisville art store by the same name, received from Charles (Carl) several small beech tree scenes to sell, each signed Charles C. Brenner. A prominent lady spied them in the window, entered and proclaimed, "Oh Mr. Lindsay, they are exquisite!" Upon closer examination, she read the signature and asked, "These are not by the sign painter, are they?" Assured they were, the sale was lost. A sign painter as an artist? At Mr. Lindsay's suggestion, Charles C. Brenner soon thereafter became Carl C. Brenner. By 1867 he had opened his own studio at 103 West Jefferson Street. Ornamental sign painting faded as landscapes of the Louisville countryside emerged.

Untitled painting by Carl Christian Brenner. *Courtesy David P. and Marilyn Taylor.*

One-time Missouri congressman, later Kentucky governor J. Proctor Knott, happened by and observed a recently completed scene of beech trees. The governor remarked, "The man that can do that well, can do better." Due to Knott's influence, Congress appropriated a significant sum to commission a painting of Brenner's beeches. It was hung in the Corcoran Gallery in Washington, D.C. The fame and recognition from this official acknowledgement of his artistic talent spread far and wide. Due to his love of the beeches, he designed and constructed a collapsible hut with glazed panels, providing him shelter from the elements and the ability to paint in all seasons. When Carl C. Brenner died on July 22, 1888, his oldest son was in Europe receiving artistic training. Knott's letter of regret stated, "His untimely taking off, just as fame and fortune were reaching out their wreaths to him, was a sad blow to me, one of the saddest of my life. Louisville and Kentucky has lost the master of the beeches." Carl Brenner is buried in Louisville's St. Louis Cemetery.

JOSEPH KREMENTZ

Joseph Krementz (1840–1928) was born to a family of eight children in Kriftel, near Frankfurt. The family immigrated to Louisville eleven years later and resided on both sides of the Ohio—in Louisville and New Albany, Indiana. From boyhood, he displayed unusual talent as an artist. At the age of nine, he was awarded first prize at an art competition in the schools of Wiesbaden. His supportive parents encouraged him to explore his talents by receiving instruction from Ludwig Knaus. His formal training was directed by German native Carl Pfetsch, a prize-winning portrait and genre painter and professional photographer active in New York, Cincinnati, Indianapolis and New Albany.

Krementz seems to have followed the path of his mentor, not only focusing on landscapes and portraits, but also incorporating photographic techniques into his art. He worked in photo studios such as Klauber's in Louisville and, for a time, owned his own business at Fourth and Jefferson Streets. Some say he earned his living by resurrecting the dead through photographs, producing a lightly printed image of someone deceased, then creating a lifelike rendition using pastel or oil.

Krementz was a close friend of Carl C. Brenner, and the camera played a part in the late years of both artists' careers. The *New Albany Tribune* reported that the two became inseparable companions, often seen together sketching scenes in southern Indiana and Kentucky. Krementz was an elder member of the Wonderland Way Art Club, a pre–World War I group of like-minded artists that was started in New Albany by James L. Russell. His art supply store and gallery became a gathering place for the Wonderland Way artists,

Summer Fields by Joseph Krementz. *Courtesy Casey and Erica Willis.*

and many exhibitions were hosted at this venue. Krementz was larger than the region, and his work was frequently exhibited in New York, Chicago, Nashville and Indianapolis. Many younger artists were nurtured in his years of involvement and dedication with the art club. Joseph Krementz passed away in April 1928 and is buried in St. Mary Cemetery in New Albany, Indiana.

PAUL PLASCHKE

Paul Albert Plaschke was born on February 2, 1880, in Berlin. The Plaschke family immigrated to the United States in 1884 through the Port of New York. Of the four artists noted in this chapter, he had the least training—none. Totally self-taught, he had remarkable success. At the age of seventeen, he informed his father that he wanted to be an artist. Wiser than some parents, his father agreed, then replied, "All right son, you're on your own, but remember, all artists starve to death." Young Plaschke forged ahead. He married Louisville native Ophelia Bennett in 1898, and in 1899 they established residence in New Albany, Indiana. He began working for the *Courier-Journal* and the *Louisville Times* drawing cartoons and caricatures six days a week. On Sundays, he added a full page of humor entitled "Local Affairs." His vocation kept him drawing, but his passion kept him painting.

Greatly influenced by the winding river valleys of Kentucky and southern Indiana, his style was a mix of plein air and Indiana impressionism. Unlike the tonalists, his impressionistic landscapes captured the beauty of the surrounding terrain with infused light and color. Friend and fellow Wonderland Way artist, Harvey Peake, noted, "No matter how lonely the place might be, when we started painting, a crowd collected to observe our work." Plaschke's study of a blue tree stirred an onlooker because he knew there were no blue trees. While looking around the site of the painters, the critic found one, admitted it and apologized. The Blanche Benjamin Memorial Prize for outstanding landscape of a southern subject was awarded to him at the Southern States Art League salon held in New Orleans in 1933. The 1934 Hoosier Salon bestowed the Indianapolis Star Prize for portraiture, another genre in which he excelled.

Paul Scott Plaschke Sr. (*left*), Emil Plaschke (*right*) and Paul Albert Plaschke (*seated*) with Paul Scott Plaschke Jr. *Courtesy Paul S. Plaschke Jr.*

Country Road by Paul Albert Plaschke. *Courtesy John and Linda Van Arsdall.*

Generosity might be a one-word definition of Plaschke. A founding member of the Wonderland Way Art Club, his efforts for the success of the organization were second only to artist, gallery owner and host, James L. Russell. Through the Wonderland Way, Plaschke guided many young artists. He and John T. Bauscher were instrumental in founding the Louisville Art Academy and taught night classes at the YMCA. Plaschke was also a founding member of the Louisville Art Association and exhibited throughout Indiana. Efforts outside the Louisville area were extensive, including showings at the Art Institute of Chicago, the National Academy of Design and the Pennsylvania Academy of Fine Arts. He was instrumental in the founding of Louisville's J.B. Speed Art Museum. Kentucky collector and philanthropist Hattie Bishop Speed purchased several of his works for the museum's permanent collection. Plaschke would later become a Speed trustee.

The great Ohio River flood of 1937 was catastrophic. His home had a basement full of water, another five feet in the living room and seven more in his studio. Many of his paintings and a lifetime collection of books were lost. It was time for change. The devastation boosted his decision to move to Chicago. He immediately went to work for the short-lived *Chicago Herald Examiner*, followed by the *Chicago Herald American* and soon became William Randolph Hearst's favorite cartoonist. A late-night phone call from Hearst describing a cartoon idea for one of his papers immediately put Plaschke to work. His finished product would be flown to the publisher's determined location, appearing in the next printing.

Retirement in 1950 brought Paul and Ophelia Plaschke back to Louisville. A new home, including studio space, provided a comfortable place to live and paint. A 1951 reunion with former student Dean Cornwell, a renowned muralist whose works are found in many public buildings and various publications, allowed student and teacher to reminisce. Cornwell recalled Plaschke's advice, "Pack your bags and go to Chicago where you can expand." Cornwell did just that and has since traveled the world, exhibiting nationwide and abroad. Plaschke fondly asked, "Aren't you glad you took my advice?" Cornwell replied, "You always were a good instructor." Paul Albert Plaschke died February 12, 1954, in Louisville and is buried in Cave Hill Cemetery.

Chapter 12

MUSIC

By F. Richard Knoop

Early Faith Foundations

In the first half of the nineteenth century, as significant numbers of Germans settled in Louisville, many established faith foundations, and there is no doubt that music played a critical role in providing hope and optimism for the faithful of these churches. The nearly simultaneous foundations of St. Paul Evangelical Church (1836) and St. Boniface Catholic Church (1837) provided opportunities for Protestant and Catholic congregations to gather and worship in German as they adapted to learning English and adopting American customs. Congregation Adas Israel (now Adath Israel) was established in 1843 to serve the Jewish community. Many other centers of worship developed, which included the Catholic churches of the Immaculate Conception of St. Mary (1845), St. Martin of Tours (1853), St. Peter (1855) and St. Joseph (1866). Church records describe choral events and activities which clearly support the festive and prayerful role of music. As expressions of art in these growing faith communities, many of the German immigrants took pride in the development of their cantors, scholas and choirs as well as in the building of beautiful organs to support worship.

In his centennial history of St. Boniface Church, published in 1937, John B. Wuest, OFM, described a grand Corpus Christi procession in 1844, which first included the sound of a bell, followed by a thundering salvo of small cannons. Then, accompanied by a German military corps in uniform, a banner appeared which waved merrily "in the free American air." To enhance its liturgies, St. Boniface Church purchased a small organ in 1841, built by Mathias Schwab of Cincinnati. That organ was replaced by a Koehnken organ in 1856, then by a Prante organ in 1891.

In 1873 an important parish event of St. Peter Evangelical Church describes the acquisition of a beautiful pipe organ. While being shipped to Louisville from New Orleans, the steamer on which the organ was being transported sank in the Mississippi River. The instrument was salvaged and renovated and, in due time, installed for use.

Some fine historical instruments still support worship in churches where German immigrants first gathered. St. Boniface Church has made great additions to its Prante organ, and there is active preservation of the Ferrand and Votey organ at St. Martin of Tours Church and the Louis Van Dinter instrument of St. Frances of Rome Church (relocated from the former Immaculate Conception of St. Mary Church).

The work of Steiner-Reck Organ Builders in the early 1960s continued to promote the Germanic style of tracker organ building, which can be seen in the organs of Comstock Hall at the University of Louisville School of Music, the Cathedral of the Assumption, and the Caldwell chapel organ of Presbyterian Theological Seminary. As Reverend Blanc of St. Boniface Church wrote in 1843 to *Der Wahrheitsfreund*, "Today the pious spirit and the soul yearning for God is transferred to the altar of the living God, carried as it were on delicate wings by the stirring tones of the organ."

GERMAN SINGING SOCIETIES

In the early years of the nineteenth century, Louisville's musical tastes were probably best served by the sentimental creations of prolific local songwriter Will S. Hays, who wrote "Mollie Darling" and "Wait for the Wagon." In 1819–20, Anton Philip Heinrich pioneered the growth of serious music in a series of concerts, and the short-lived St. Cecilia Society was founded in 1822. In order to promote unity among the German immigrants in the community, as well as a preservation of history and culture, the Liederkranz Society was founded in 1848. The following year, the Mozart Society was organized and presented concerts in Mozart Hall, at Fourth and Jefferson Streets. The hall became the center of the city's musical life until the Mozart Society was disbanded during the Civil War.

Social Male Chorus, 1943. *Courtesy German-American Club Gesangverein.*

The founding of the Liederkranz Society led to the formation of a Nord-Amerikanischer Sängerbund (North American Singing Society) in 1849. Louisville hosted the second Sängerfest (singing festival) of the society in 1850. In 1849, the Orpheus Choral Society grew in prominence among Louisville groups, and in 1865 the Singing Federation of Louisville was founded, comprising the Liederkranz, Orpheus and Frohsinn singing groups. In 1873, the first Liederkranz Hall, located on Market Street, was completed and served as a center of German social life.

The Social Male Chorus was founded in 1878 by Louis Vormbrock at Beck's Hall on Jefferson Street. The fifteen men who met there called themselves the Sozialer Männerchor. Otto Schuler directed the choir, and their first concert was performed at the gardens of Beck's Hall in June 1879. This choral group advanced in 1884 to form a constitution and develop a society flag. For two decades, Professor Gustav Clausnitzer directed this choir, leading them to many national Sängerfeste (singing festivals). In 1937 a Ladies Auxiliary was formed, but women were not admitted to full membership until 1992, when the organization changed its name to the German-American Club Gesangverein. Although as many as twenty German singing societies existed in Louisville's history, the German-American Club Gesangverein is the only one remaining.

THE LOUISVILLE PHILHARMONIC SOCIETY

German influence was felt even more strongly after the Civil War when the Louisville Philharmonic Society was organized in 1866. The society's orchestra (all amateur musicians) was conducted by Louis Henry Hast. Hast was born in Gochlinger, Bavaria, on January 13, 1822. Upon his graduation from the Munich Conservatory of Music, he and his brother Jacob, an artist, came to Bardstown, Kentucky, where they lived until Jacob's death. Louis's musical talent was quickly recognized, and he served as the first organist at the old St. Louis Church on Fifth Street, now the site of the Cathedral of the Assumption. After Hast's elopement and marriage to Emma Sorgenfrey Wilder in 1860, their home became a center of musical activity. Hast's reputation as a fine music teacher helped to strengthen the quality of the society, and many fine German musicians comprised the orchestra. Louis Hast also served as director of La Reunion Musicale, the Philharmonic Society and the Mozart Society. One of his most accomplished pupils was Hattie Bishop Speed. After traveling to Germany in the late 1880s, Hast suffered attacks of vertigo that sent him into a deep depression. He took his own life in a shop in downtown Louisville on February 12, 1890, and is interred at Cave Hill Cemetery.

Soon after the death of Louis Henry Hast, Karl "Papa" Schmidt, a much-loved cellist and composer, relocated to Louisville from a teaching position at Torrington College in Toronto, Ontario, in Canada. Karl Schmidt was born in Schwerin, Mecklenburg, and began playing cello and piano at a young age. After graduating from the Leipzig Conservatory, he performed as a solo cellist for composer Johann Strauss in Vienna. He appeared as a soloist and conductor with the Municipal Theatre in Zürich, Switzerland, and as conductor of the English Grand Opera Company. During his time in Europe, Schmidt performed under Johannes Brahms, Anton Rubinstein, Arthur Nikisch, Franz Liszt, Anton Seidl and Dr. Hans Von Bulow. Upon his arrival in Louisville in 1891, he directed the Liederkranz Society and the Philharmonic Orchestra. In the same year, he became the cellist for the Burch Quintette and began to serve as the organist and choirmaster of Temple Adath Israel, a position he held for fifty years. From 1906 to 1908, Schmidt directed the Henry W. Savage Opera Company in New York. His work included conducting productions of *Madame Butterfly* (Puccini) and *The Merry Widow* (Lehar) in Madison Square Garden. Upon his return to Louisville from New York in 1908, he began teaching at the Conservatory of Music in Louisville as a private cello instructor and served as soloist and

Above: Louisville Philharmonic Society, early 1900s. *Courtesy New Albany–Floyd County Public Library.*

Right: Karl Schmidt. *Courtesy University of Louisville Photographic Archives.*

musical director at the WHAS radio station. Following these appointments, he became the chair of the advanced music theory program and artist in residence of the cello faculty of the University of Louisville School of Music. In 1930 Schmidt was awarded the David Bispham Memorial Medal by the American Opera Society for his American grand opera entitled *The Lady of the Lake*, a vocal score published in Chicago. Prior to his death on October 7, 1950, Schmidt completed an oratorio, *Judas*, which was performed in Louisville in the 1990s.

Moritz von Bomhard and the Kentucky Opera Association

Liederkranz Hall, built by the Liederkranz Society, was used frequently by touring opera companies and especially by German-language theatrical troupes in the last quarter of the nineteenth century. As vocal music in Louisville reached new heights in the first half of the twentieth century, Moritz von Bomhard, a conductor, opera producer, composer and pianist, had a profound influence. Bomhard, born in Munich, Germany, on June 19, 1908, was the son of Johanna and Ernst von Bomhard, an industrial engineer. While he studied law at the University of Leipzig, he simultaneously received a diploma in music from the Leipzig Conservatory. In Leipzig, Bomhard met and married Leila Atkinson, a Kentucky-born cellist. After settling in New York in 1935, the aspiring young musician and conductor studied at the Juilliard School and accepted a teaching position at Princeton University in 1937. This first music appointment, which included conducting the university's orchestra and glee club, provided time for Bomhard to compose three symphonies, a concerto for strings and several pieces of chamber, piano and vocal music. Like many young music educators, Bomhard supplemented his income by coaching singers and groups while offering private piano instruction.

While serving in the United States Army during World War II, Bomhard became an American citizen in 1942. His wife, Leila, developed a mental illness that led to her hospitalization and death in 1945. In 1949 Bomhard was invited to Louisville by Fletcher Smith, the chair of the Voice Department at the University of Louisville School of Music, with whom he had studied at Juilliard to produce a student opera. Bomhard chose Mozart's *The Marriage of Figaro*, and it proved a great triumph for Bomhard, the university and the

Moritz von Bomhard. *Courtesy University of Louisville Photographic Archives.*

Louisville musical arts community. In 1950 and 1951, Bomhard returned to produce Menotti's *The Old Maid and the Thief* and Puccini's *Gianni Schicchi*. The enthusiasm of the Louisville public following the performance of *The Marriage of Figaro* led Bomhard to disband his New Lyric Stage troupe. He settled in Louisville, where he and a group of citizens founded the Kentucky Opera Association in 1952.

Unlike many European opera companies that were founded by royal families, the Kentucky Opera Association's backers included prominent citizens who donated large sums as well as many dedicated citizens of lesser means who provided moral support. Such energetic support continues to this day. The Kentucky Opera Association currently ranks as the twelfth-oldest regional opera company in the United States. Bomhard possessed tremendous talent for many aspects of leading this new company. His travels to New York allowed him to hear and cast young singers who went on to achieve international recognition. One notable mezzo-soprano, Taryana Troyanos, sang her first *Carmen* with the Kentucky Opera Association.

Bomhard's great talent for composition, as well as his other musical attributes, encouraged his involvement in cultivating the total art of producing opera. In the early days of production, he could be found painting the sets in addition to overseeing their design. His tireless drive to educate the public never faded as he worked to create concerts featuring what were known as bread-and-butter lyric dramas. These creative pursuits included Puccini's *La Bohème*, Verdi's *Traviata* and Bizet's *Carmen*. Under Bomhard's leadership as a German American, he also recognized the need to occasionally translate opera texts into English. His ultimate goal was always to invite people into this glorious art form. Another element of success in the development of opera under Bomhard was his partnership with the Louisville Philharmonic Society orchestra, as this company produced and recorded five new operas in English. Aside from a short leave to work with the Hamburg State Opera, Bomhard served in management of the Kentucky Opera Association until his retirement in 1982. The opening of the Kentucky Center for the Arts in 1983 heralded a new 622-seat theater named in his honor. In 1984 his second wife, mezzo-soprano Charme Riesley, died, and he never fully recovered from this loss. After returning to Germany in 1994 to be with his remaining family, Bomhard settled in Salzburg, Austria, where he died on July 23, 1996. He is buried in the family tomb in Munich, Germany. Bomhard and conductors who succeeded him have continued to develop programs that educate youth and the general public to the wonder of opera. The German American spirit of this great musician and conductor continues to enliven the operatic stage of Louisville.

GERHARD HERZ

No discussion of the German influence in Louisville music would be complete without a reflection on the many contributions of Gerhard Herz. A world-renowned Bach scholar and beloved teacher for forty years at the University of Louisville, his impact continues throughout the musical world in his many publications. Dr. Herz was born to a Jewish family in Düsseldorf, Germany, in 1911. With the assistance of humanitarian Albert

Schweitzer, he and his family escaped Nazi Germany in 1938. Dr. Herz earned his PhD from the University of Zürich, and this accomplishment, along with several letters from Dr. Schweitzer, helped him to secure a faculty position at the University of Louisville. After founding the Music History Department in the College of Arts and Sciences in 1956, he served as its chair until his retirement in 1978.

After his arrival at the University of Louisville, Dr. Herz married Mary Jo Fink (1916–95), an Ohio native and Phi Beta Kappa graduate of Ohio State University, who taught French at the University of Louisville from 1942 to 1979. As an educator, Dr. Herz demonstrated a vibrant love for teaching through countless university-sponsored seminars. He engaged

Gerhard Herz. *Courtesy University of Louisville Photographic Archives.*

students with wit and humor and truly energized the musical life of Louisville. As cofounder of the Chamber Music Society, Dr. Herz served for more than twenty years on the board of the Louisville Orchestra and served faithfully as a founding board member of the Louisville Bach Society.

Dr. Herz was instrumental in convincing Dmitri Shostakovich, a leading musical figure of the Soviet Union, to visit Louisville in 1959. This virtuoso's visit was part of a goodwill tour at the height of the Cold War, and Shostakovich went on to become one of the most celebrated composers of the twentieth century. Herz also helped to bring the world-renowned Budapest String Quartet to Louisville in 1961.

Dr. Herz was the founder and the first chairman of the American chapter of the New Bach Society—now the American Bach Society. In 1984 he published a four-hundred-page book entitled *Bach Sources in America* in both German and English. As a reference catalog, this book sources more than twenty locations through the United States. The collection of Gerhard Herz at the Dwight Anderson Music Library at the University of Louisville includes lecture notes, awards, research and correspondence dating from the early 1960s to 1990. The collection consists of thirty feet of papers compiled through Dr. Herz's passion to blend scholarship and musical performance in the Louisville community. Dr. Gerhard Herz died at age eighty-eight on September 3, 2000.

THE LOUISVILLE BACH SOCIETY

The Germanic influence of composer Johann Sebastian Bach soared to new heights through the creative pursuits of Melvin and Margaret Leupold Dickinson, who founded the Louisville Bach Society in 1964. Their inspiration for this organization grew after meeting as Fulbright scholars in the late 1950s in Frankfurt-am-Main, where they studied with the world-renowned Bach expert Helmut Walcha. After a courtship of several years, the two friends married in 1961. Together, they embraced the musical wealth of Bach and determined that his cantatas should be brought to the people of Kentucky.

Melvin Dickinson was the head of the Organ and Church Music Department at the University of Louisville School of Music for forty-two years, retiring as professor emeritus in 2001. Margaret Dickinson graduated from the Oberlin Conservatory of Music and the Ohio State University. While Melvin was at the University of Louisville, Margaret taught church service playing and harpsichord literature at the collegiate level and organ at the preparatory level. Both Dickinsons volunteered decades of service to the music of Calvary Episcopal Church.

The Louisville Bach Society specialized in performing the world of J.S. Bach as well as the choral masterpieces of Handel, Haydn, Mozart, Brahms and others. The society also took bold steps to include some of the leading contemporary composers. The Dickinsons were strong advocates of performing works seldom performed in Louisville. Their work led to presentations of Bach's *Mass in B Minor* and *St. Matthew Passion*, Mozart's *C Minor Mass*, Beethoven's *Missa Solemnis* and Bruckner's *F Minor Mass*.

Singers in the Louisville Bach Society came from many areas and occupations and included surgeons, bishops, music teachers, students, attorneys, social workers and nurses. All were drawn by their common love for the music of Bach and the desire to provide excellence in choral singing. Great care was taken in selecting performance venues that would truly highlight the total breadth of these great masterpieces. The Louisville public was introduced to the architecture of great Louisville churches at Calvary Episcopal Church, St. Agnes Church, Holy Spirit Church, Second Presbyterian Church and Harvey Brown Presbyterian Church. Other venues included the Kentucky Center for the Arts, the Macauley Theatre (Brown Theatre) and the University of Louisville's Comstock North Recital Hall. Through the generosity of Louisville benefactors Mary and Barry Bingham Sr., in 1988 a five-year project for the performance of a complete *Messiah*

Louisville Bach Society. *Courtesy Louisville Bach Society.*

was presented as a gift to the Louisville community. The Binghams were very generous in supporting this society, and on February 22, 1998, a concert was performed in Holy Spirit Church to memorialize their generosity.

For nearly fifty years, the Bach society served as a true landmark in Louisville's cultural landscape until a final performance of Bach's *Mass in B Minor* (BWV 232) on May 1, 2011. Melvin and Margaret Dickinson raised the bar for choral and organ music in Louisville as they brought great choral works to local stages and church sanctuaries. They continued to provide musical outreach from their home with an organ musical performance series featuring the organ works of J.S. Bach and Dietrich Buxtehude. Melvin Dickinson, a great force in Louisville's classical community, died on January 31, 2014, at his home. A memorial service was held on February 8 at Calvary Episcopal Church, at which many of his students played and offered choral tribute. Margaret Dickinson continues to share her musical gifts as a highly respected organist in the Louisville community.

Chapter 13

GERMANS IN SOUTHERN INDIANA

By Carl E. Kramer

Germans have played vital roles in the social, economic, religious and political life of southern Indiana since the earliest days of European settlement. By 1820 several German families had settled within the present boundaries of Clark, Floyd and Harrison Counties, which border Louisville and Jefferson County, Kentucky. Their numbers exploded between 1830 and the Civil War. It is difficult to determine precisely how German immigrants came to southern Indiana, but most of them likely sailed from northern German and western European ports, arrived on the East Coast or New Orleans and traveled by steamboats along the inland waterway system to the Falls of the Ohio River. Many settled in Louisville and then crossed the river. Most settled in Jeffersonville or New Albany, but others found homes in smaller interior communities or on outlying farms. Their homeland roots were diverse, but they quickly made their presence felt.

The Germans had varied occupations. They included merchants, professionals, manufacturers, tradesmen and laborers. Many became prominent in their fields, and some established businesses that passed through multiple generations. Charles A. Schimpff, a native of Bavaria, immigrated as a child in 1850 and eventually settled in Jeffersonville, where he became a dealer of books, wallpaper and stationery. His brother, Gustav A. Schimpff, opened a confectionery in 1891, and Schimpff's Confectionery still operates under family ownership. Wainwright George J. Holzbog emigrated from Germany to Jeffersonville and organized a wagon manufacturing firm that later passed to his son, George H. Holzbog. Abraham Schwaninger, a Swiss immigrant, was prominent in political and business circles, and his sons, Charles A. and Willacy J. Schwaninger, made their marks in the pharmacy business. Peter F. Myers, whose father was born to German parents in New York, was born in Jeffersonville and established a lumber business that lasted for several generations. Peter's younger brother, Newton H. Myers, established a successful business producing wagons, kitchen cabinets and household supplies.

Many Germans entered agricultural processing businesses. Seeing Jeffersonville's German population as a market for beer, Peter Bieson and Henry Lang opened breweries that supplied local saloons, many operated by Germans. Taking advantage of the proximity to Louisville's Bourbon Stockyards, John L. Rockstroh produced lard, oil and candles. In 1869 George Pfau began processing animal oils on the riverfront, and the George Pfau's Sons Company is now in its fifth generation.

In the professional arena, George H. Voigt, the son of immigrants Ferdinand and Eva K. Voight, studied law at the University of Louisville, became a prominent attorney and acquired the *National Democrat* and the *Evening News*. His son, George H. Voigt Jr., and his grandson, Owen Voigt,

Warren and Jill Schimpff pouring red hots. *Courtesy Schimpff's Confectionery.*

George Pfau. *Courtesy George Pfau's Sons Company.*

followed his lead in both law and publishing. Similarly, Swiss immigrant John C. Zulauf studied law at the University of Louisville, established a successful legal practice, entered the banking industry and was a prominent transportation promotor.

Germans also figured prominently in New Albany, one of Indiana's largest cities before the Civil War, and many became leaders in business and industry. John Gadient, August Barth and George A. Moser established tanneries that lasted for several generations. John F. Gebhard, born in Pennsylvania to German parents, established the New Albany Woolen and Cotton Mills, which grew into the largest textile concern in the Midwest. He was also an influential railroad, bridge and utility promoter in the late nineteenth century. With backing from industrialist Washington C. DePauw, machinist Charles Hegewald, a native of Saxony, organized the New Albany Machine Manufacturing Company, which produced machine and marine engines. Immigrant Paul Reising opened the Paul Reising Brewing Company in 1855 and bottled beers with names like *Rathskeller Brew, Kaiser, Imperial Pale* and *Culmbacher.* Klerner Furniture Company, formed about

1858 by Henry Klerner, manufactured bedroom suites and other items, most of which were shipped to stores in New York. The company later passed to his son Peter. Andreas Danz established a soap factory that passed on to his son Charles.

Many Germans also made their marks as professionals and tradesmen. Christopher Heimberger established a successful photography business; Jacob Loesch, a native of Prussia, operated a blacksmith shop; Fred Maetschke and H.G. Harmeling conducted a tailoring business, as did John Hieb. Adam Sohn, John Diebold and Edward Crumbo were well known stone masons; carpenter George Helfrich operated a planing mill and lumberyard; Andrew Miller and his son conducted a plumbing business. Immigrant Albert Schindler pursued the plastering trade and passed the business to his son, Charles W. Schindler, who eventually gave up the trade and became a teacher. Andros Huncilman, the eldest son of Austrian immigrant Mathias Huncilman, became a successful real estate dealer and residential developer. His son, James J. Huncilman, was a surveyor and contractor who built many streets and sewer lines. He reputedly surveyed Louisville and New Albany to create the Louisville, New Albany and St. Louis Railroad tunnel through Edwardsville Hill. Louis Hammersmith, who was born in Germany in 1852, entered the freight business with his father and later operated the Louisville and New Albany Freight Transfer Line. One of the city's most vigorous German entrepreneurs was Frederick Wunderlich. He came to the United States in 1848 and settled in Louisville in 1852. There, he produced boots and shoes before moving to New Albany. During the next decade, he pursued the wholesale grocery business and successively expanded into the livestock trade; food, grain and commission business; and wholesale liquor distribution.

While most Germans gravitated to the larger towns of Jeffersonville and New Albany, many settled in rural areas and small towns in the hinterlands of Clark, Floyd and Harrison Counties. In some cases, Germans became town planners in their own right. Large Pennsylvania Dutch clans, such as the George W. Swartz and Nicholas Lentz families, and immigrant families like those of Peter Deibel and Henry J. Lutz, arrived in Utica Township during the early nineteenth century and established multi-generation farms that operated well into the twentieth century. Some members of these families ventured into other fields. For example, Allen A. Swartz organized a successful Jeffersonville dry goods store in 1878. In neighboring Silver Creek Township, immigrant families like those of William Dreyer, Philip Jacob Kramer, Frederic Loheide and Louis Utrecht established farms in the vicinity of Sellersburg, Speed, Hamburg and Jacob's Chapel. John Scheller, a native of Bavaria, was an influential farmer, grocer, real estate dealer and land developer in Sellersburg, while Albert Diefenbach operated a cattle farm and conducted a farm implement and hardware business in Sellersburg.

Elsewhere in the county, Louis Spriestersbach, the son of German immigrants George and Eva Spriestersbach, operated a large farm in Charlestown Township and was associated with his brother Julius in several businesses in Charlestown. James D. Kiger, a grandson of German immigrant Joseph Kiger, married a daughter of Louis Spriestersbach, opened a hardware store in Charlestown and raised livestock on a nearby farm. Immigrants Jacob and Barbara Deuser bought a farm in Charlestown Township and later passed it on to their son, William M. Deuser, who also operated a hardware business in Louisville. In 1853 Conrad Eberts Sr. arrived in the United States with his sons, Jacob and Conrad Jr. In the 1870s the brothers arrived in Henryville, Indiana, where they bought a flour mill. It burned down several years later, but the brothers rebuilt and established mills in Charlestown and Jeffersonville.

Germans were prominent in the creation of two communities in western Clark County. During the 1840s and 1850s, families headed by Simon Huber, Jacob Stumler, John Koetter, William Book, John A. Rosenberger, Henry Hanka and Henry Kruer settled in the Knobs of southeast Wood Township. They prospered as farmers and fruit growers and established a tight-knit community based on intermarriage and devotion to Roman Catholicism. The community became known as Starlight in 1892. In 1959 Thomas Koetter, a descendant of one of Starlight's pioneer families, started Koetter Woodworking, and during the next six decades, it grew into a large woodworking and construction business. About six miles to the east, near the boundary of Silver Creek and Carr Townships, the families of Peter Paul Renn, Peter Biesel, Philip Strobel, Martin Koerner, Joseph Ehringer and Joseph Popp settled around St. Joseph and began growing berries and fruit, which they shipped to distant markets like Chicago via the Monon Railroad.

Germans also settled in rural Floyd County. One of the first arrivals was John Tresenriter, a Pennsylvania Dutchman who settled in Georgetown Township in 1818. More people moved to nearby Floyd's Knobs, which attracted members of families from Starlight. Joining them were families with names like Becht, Buechler, Moser, Freiberger, Banet, Andres, Best, Englemann, Zimmerman and Kirchgessner. Like those in St.

Joseph and Starlight, Germans in Floyd's Knobs became producers of fruits and vegetables.

Harrison County was not as heavily populated as Clark and Floyd Counties, but Germans made their presence felt. Immigrant John Peter Mauck opened the area's first Ohio River ferry operation opposite Brandenburg, Kentucky, in 1811. His son, Fredrick Mauck, platted Mauckport in 1827. John Anschutz, a native of Saxony, arrived in Louisville before the Civil War and later bought a farm near Buena Vista. Noah Elbert, born in Germany in 1838, was located in Harrison County after the Civil War and established himself as a stonecutter, sawmill operator and farmer. David Lemmel, born in Louisville of German parents, became a prosperous strawberry farmer. Germans were also leaders in settling the towns of New Middletown and Lanesville.

Regardless of where they settled, Germans eager to perpetuate their "Germanness" brought many of their social and cultural practices with them. Foremost among them was their religion, and immigrants quickly set about organizing churches, which became centers of religious, social and educational life. The first Protestant congregation was the forerunner of the present St. Mark United Church of Christ in New Albany. It was organized in 1837 under the pastoral leadership of the Reverend Henry Evers and the lay administration of President John Pleiss, Secretary John Radecke and Treasurer Henry Kohl. The congregation first met in a school on State Street between the Ohio River and Main Street. The church was formally chartered as the German Evangelical, Lutheran and Reformed Church of New Albany, Indiana, in 1843. After worshipping at several temporary locations, the congregation dedicated a new Gothic Revival edifice in 1870 and adopted the name St. Mark Evangelical Church in 1921, after the suspension of German language services.

Jeffersonville Protestants with a similar theological perspective began meeting in January 1860. They bought the former First Presbyterian Church in June, and in 1861 they organized the First German United Lutheran and Reformed Congregation in Jeffersonville. The congregation began with forty-one charter members. The first pastor was the Reverend John F. Grassow, a Prussian-born Lutheran who served until August 1862. He was succeeded by Reverend Hartley, and the congregation changed its name to the German Evangelical St. Luke Church. St. Luke's dedicated its current Gothic Revival structure in 1915. Today, the congregation is known as St. Luke United Church of Christ. Germans in Silver Creek Township, led by the Reverend J.H. Krueger, formed St. Paul Reformed

St. Mark Evangelical Church, 1911. *Courtesy New Albany–Floyd County Public Library.*

Church in 1871. Soon thereafter, the members approved a constitution and erected a small frame church in downtown Sellersburg, where they worshipped until 1969, when they occupied a new edifice in Hamburg. The congregation became St. Paul United Church of Christ. The church struggled with low membership, and it finally closed in the 1990s. Meanwhile, Evangelical Germans in Harrison County organized the German Evangelical Reformed Peace Church in New Middletown; today it is Salem United Church of Christ.

Not all German Protestants adhered to Evangelical and Reformed doctrines. In 1825, German families in Greenville Township established St. John Lutheran Church with Reverend Glenn as the organizing pastor. In 1845 Jeffersonville Germans of Wesleyan persuasion organized the German Methodist Episcopal Church under the Reverend Conrad Muth. Five years later, led by Reverend Heller, countrymen in New Albany organized a German Methodist Episcopal Church. After meeting for several years in private homes and then in a schoolhouse, they built a permanent brick edifice at Fifth and Spring Streets. In neighboring Harrison County, Germans organized St. Peter Lutheran Church in Corydon in 1852.

German Catholics were equally as eager to establish their faith in southern Indiana. During the early settlement period, German Catholics

St. Luke Evangelical Church, 1937. *Courtesy St. Luke United Church of Christ.*

often worshipped in multi-ethnic parishes, usually consisting of German, Irish and French families. As early as 1820, Catholics in the vicinity of Galena in Floyd County began worshipping in a log cabin located on Little Indian Creek. In 1823 they organized St. Mary of the Knobs Church, and in about 1837 they erected a new edifice, with Mass served by Reverend Louis Neyron, a French-born priest. Three years later, Reverend Neyron spearheaded the organization of St. Mary Church in Greenville, composed largely of German and French settlers. Holy Trinity Church in New Albany was established in 1837 for an Irish and German congregation. Although the congregation served almost even numbers of Irish and Germans, the latter wanted their own parish. By 1854 organization and planning for St. Mary of the Annunciation Catholic Church began and proceeded for the next five years. In 1859 the congregation dedicated its Gothic Revival edifice at the northwest corner of Spring and Eighth Streets.

Organization of Catholic parishes in Clark County followed a somewhat similar pattern as in Floyd County. Visiting priests celebrated Mass in Jeffersonville until 1850, when a Mass conducted by Reverend Daniel Maloney inspired a German, Leopold Zapf, to begin raising funds to build a chapel. It was dedicated as St. Anthony of Padua in 1851. The congregation and the building grew rapidly during the ministry of Reverend Augustine Bessonies and his successors. St. Anthony of Padua Church served a predominantly German congregation in Jeffersonville until 1949, when it moved to nearby Clarksville. Reverend Neyron and Reverend Bessonies, among others, also ministered to German Catholics at St. Joseph during the late 1840s and 1850s. In 1853 the settlers built a small frame church that served the parish until the dedication of the magnificent Gothic Revival edifice that crowns St. Joseph Hill today. Meanwhile, Germans were instrumental in organizing St. Michael Church in Charlestown, St. Francis Xavier Church in Henryville and St. John the Baptist Church in Starlight during the 1860s. Although Germans were less numerous in Harrison County, in 1849 Catholics organized St. Bernard Church in Depauw and St. Peter Church in Elizabeth, the Church of Most Precious Blood in New Middletown in 1880 and St. Joseph Church in Corydon in 1896.

Whether Protestant or Catholic, German churches served as centers of community life. Virtually all operated parochial schools, which perpetuated German culture and language while inculcating religious beliefs and values. Many men in St. Anthony's joined St. George Commandery of the Knights of St. John, a semi-military social order for German Catholics. St. Mark's, St. Luke's and St. Paul's had men's groups that offered fellowship and entertainment opportunities and Ladies Aid Societies that assisted families of deceased members and enabled women to lead important ministries at a time when church governance functions were controlled by men.

Germans conducted a variety of other educational, cultural and athletic programs and activities of a secular nature. One of Louisville's first German newspapers, *Der Beobachter am Ohio*, was established in 1844 and edited by a Jeffersonville resident, Heinrich Beutel, and was circulated on both sides of the Ohio River. Rudolph Schimpff, a son of Charles A. Schimpff, became a journalist and established a paper called the *Jeffersonville Star*. Three German-language newspapers appeared in New Albany, beginning with the short-lived *Sonne* in the early 1850s. The *New Albany Democrat* appeared in 1861 and lasted for about six months, and the *Deutsche Zeitung* was started in 1875 and continued for several years.

Professor Paul Moosmiller organized the Independent German-American School in 1866, initiated construction in 1867 and deeded the completed structure to the New Albany City Schools in 1871. After the Civil War, the Männerchor Hall in New Albany became a popular venue for presentations

Above: St. Mary of the Annunciation Catholic Church, 1905. *Courtesy New Albany–Floyd County Public Library.*

Left: St. Anthony of Padua Catholic Church. *Courtesy St. Anthony of Padua Church.*

of oratorios, chorales, recitals and other musical programs. The Jeffersonville Sängerbund, a singing society that drew men from both Protestant and Catholic churches, participated in state, regional and national singing competitions during the late nineteenth and early twentieth centuries. Bandsman and composer Henry Dreyer played for John Philip Sousa, then conducted a popular youth band program in New Albany during the early twentieth century. In the late 1870s, Germans in Jeffersonville joined members of other ethnic groups in walking competitions over a course that followed several city blocks for a distance of two miles. The walking contests were a short-lived fad. Longer lasting was the Turnverein movement, which brought physical culture activities to New Albany.

Like immigrants in Louisville and elsewhere, Germans in southern Indiana were affected by and participated in the major national events of the day. During the 1850s, Germans were targets of a particularly virulent strain of political nativism that exploited white Americans' fears of immigrants, Catholics and radicals. This was called the "Know-Nothing" movement because its members espoused secrecy. Indiana's first Know-Nothing lodge was formed in Lawrenceburg in early 1854, and within months the virus had infected the entire state under the banner of the American Party.

Jeffersonville and New Albany became nativist hotbeds, and like Louisville in 1855, both cities suffered election-day riots on October 10, 1854, as nativists attempted to prevent German and Irish immigrants from voting. No serious injuries occurred in Jeffersonville, and within a short time, a sense of calm had returned to the city. The scene was more violent in New Albany, where a "Fusionist" ticket composed of Know-Nothings and former Whigs challenged the prevailing Democrats. Egged on by the *New Albany Tribune*, Know-Nothings brutally assaulted German and Irish immigrants who were attempting to exercise the right to vote. Fights lasted into the night, and several people, mostly Irish, were beaten and severely injured. The Know-Nothing violence enabled the Fusionists to carry the day, but the victory was ephemeral, as Democrat Ashbel P. Willard, a New Albany lawyer and Indiana lieutenant governor, ousted the Fusionists in 1856 during his campaign for governor.

The calm that followed the Know-Nothing riots was shattered in 1861 with the outbreak of the Civil War, when Germans throughout southern Indiana joined the fight to save the Union and abolish slavery. Unlike Louisville, where many Germans enlisted in companies of their own— including some based in Indiana—most southern Indiana Germans joined up with their neighbors, regardless of ethnicity, and few stood out as officers.

Independent German-American School, 1945. *Courtesy New Albany–Floyd County Public Library.*

There were exceptions, however. In Clark County, Captain Benjamin Lutz recruited a company from the Charlestown area that was incorporated into a brigade of the Indiana Legion, created by the state of Indiana to help protect the state's southern border. More noteworthy were three German companies organized in Floyd County: the National Guard unit led by Captain John P. Frank, the German Artillery commanded by Captain Knapp and the Steuben Guard headed by Captain Fred Pistorious. The lieutenants in all three companies also were German.

Anti-German sentiment emerged again during World War I, when many Americans feared that German descendants favored Germany. To the contrary, scores of men of German descent flocked to the colors. The women at St. Mark Evangelical Church organized a Red Cross sewing unit, the congregation hosted patriotic meetings and members were active in Liberty Bond drives. Nevertheless, Germans and their institutions faced an anti-German backlash. New Albany High School temporarily stopped teaching German, and St. Mark's, St. Luke's and St. Paul's finally ceased the use of German language in their parochial schools and Sunday worship.

Despite the World War I hysteria, Germans became increasingly integrated into community life, including politics and government, during the late nineteenth and early twentieth centuries. They participated in both political parties, and many won public office. Democrat Herman Preefer was mayor of Jeffersonville from 1885 to 1887, Republican Abraham Schwaninger served from 1902 to 1904, Democrat Ernest W. Rauth served from 1914 to 1917 and Republican Newton H. Myers followed him and served until 1921. Democrat Richard L. Vissing was elected in 1964 and served for twenty years, the longest tenure in the city's history. Democrat Thomas Kunkle was elected mayor of New Albany in 1871 and died in office. Democrat William A. Broecker served from 1892 to 1894, Democrat Edward Crumbo served from 1898 to 1902 and was succeeded by Republican Frank L. Shrader, who remained until 1904. Democrat Jacob G. Hauswald served from 1936 through 1939, and Garnett "Tuffy" Inman served from 1964 to 1971.

One of Harrison County's most prominent politicians was Strother M. Stockslager. Born in Mauckport, he was a Union States Army captain in the Civil War, practiced law in Corydon and was elected to the Indiana Senate and then the U.S. House of Representatives. Many other German descendants, especially among the Knobs clans, have served and continue to hold various county offices.

Chapter 14

PORTRAITS OF TWENTIETH-CENTURY IMMIGRANTS

By C. Robert Ullrich, Victoria A. Ullrich
and Patricia Boeckmann Stout

In the decade following World War I, 386,634 Germans immigrated to the United States following the economic collapse of Germany. After World War II, 576,905 Germans came to the United States following the destruction of their homeland during the war.

In this chapter, portraits of four twentieth-century German immigrants are presented to illustrate the ongoing contributions of Germans to America and to Louisville in particular. Two were prominent members of the Social Male Chorus—a German singing society now known as the German-American Club Gesangverein, one was the person most responsible for the city of Mainz becoming Louisville's German sister city and the fourth was a world-class figure skater who settled in Louisville.

AUGUST BOECKMANN

August Bernhard Boeckmann was born in Mühlen, Oldenburg, on July 18, 1906. "Gus," as he was later known, was the youngest of six children born to August Clemens and Paulina Rüwe Böckmann and was raised on a farm. Although he loved his life in Mühlen, he wanted to pursue a career other than farming. It was then that he made the decision to study tailoring and learned the trade from a friend of the family.

In 1927 Gus decided to visit his two older sisters, Johanna and Mia, who had already immigrated to the United States. On October 7, 1927, he arrived at the Port of New York aboard the *George Washington* and was met by his sister Mia and her husband, Henry Boeckmann, who took him to Cincinnati, Ohio, where they resided.

After a few weeks in Cincinnati, Gus knew he wanted to stay in the United States, so he looked for work as a tailor. Unfortunately, jobs in his field of expertise were hard to find, so he took a job selling insurance for Metropolitan Insurance Company.

August Boeckmann. *Courtesy Patricia Boeckmann Stout.*

Cincinnati was a hub of German immigration, especially for those from northern Germany, and Gus loved the city and the many friends he acquired. Like so many Germans from his area in Germany, he loved music and singing, so it seemed fitting that he would join one of the German singing societies in Cincinnati as well as the Kolping Society. Cincinnati and the German societies were the cure for the homesickness he felt for his beloved Germany.

Cincinnati was also where Gus met his future wife, Odelia Wuebker, who was of German descent and was from St. Henry, Ohio. Upon meeting Odelia (known as Dee), Gus said that he knew she was the one when she started speaking to him in his native Plattdeutsch.

On March 1, 1930, Gus and Dee married and settled in Cincinnati. In March 1931, their son August Frederick was born, and in December 1936, their second son, Richard, joined the family. Gus was still selling insurance but decided he needed to pursue his tailoring career, so the family moved to Kentucky, where he was offered a job as a "master tailor and designer" for the Lee-McClain Company in Shelbyville. At that time, Americans were still a little skeptical of Germans, especially in a small town in Kentucky. It was remembered that upon Gus's arrival at the Lee-McClain Company, an employee was looking out the window of the factory and saw Gus pull up in his car. She informed her fellow employees that the new boss was going to be okay because he had an American flag on the bumper of his car. On March 8, 1943, Gus officially became a proud citizen of the United States of America, but he never wavered in his love for his homeland.

In Shelbyville, Gus and Dee welcomed two more children, Carolyn in 1942 and James in 1943. They eventually moved to Louisville for two reasons: a Catholic education for their children and membership in the Social Male Chorus. Their last child, Patricia, completed the family in 1950. Gus continued to be an employee of Lee-McClain until he retired in 1983.

The Social Male Chorus, like the clubs in Cincinnati, provided Gus with familiar memories of Germany. He joined the club in the late 1940s and was an active member for the rest of his life. He was president of the club for six years in the 1950s and 1960s, most notably on the occasion of its seventy-fifth anniversary in 1953.

Dee served as president of the Ladies Auxiliary of the club for several years and as kitchen manager despite having five children in tow. Both Gus and Dee were members of the singing groups at the club from the start of their memberships until their health prevented them from participating. Dee passed away on February 11, 1989, and Gus died on March 31, 2000.

Gus's contributions to the Social Male Chorus were immeasurable, and his legacy lives on through his children, two of whom were presidents of the club. His son James served the longest, twenty-five years, and his daughter Patricia was the first female president.

Marta Dietrich Edie

Marta Liesel Dietrich was born on February 21, 1926, in Diez an der Lahn, near Limburg in Hessen-Nassau. As a young woman, she loved to travel to the nearby cities to shop. She was especially fond of Mainz—a love that would later blossom into a civic relationship.

Marta Dietrich married Dayton Edie, a career U.S. Army serviceman, in Frankfurt am Main on April 28, 1950. He was born in Cincinnati, Ohio, on February 9, 1925, and lived in Pendleton County, Kentucky, during his youth. He served in the Battle of the Bulge in World War II and in the Korean conflict and was a Purple Heart recipient.

Marta Dietrich Edie immigrated to the United States in 1950, arriving at the Port of New York aboard the *George W. Goethals* on August 9. Dayton and Marta Edie initially settled in San Francisco, California, where he was stationed in the army. While living in San Francisco in 1951, they had a son,

Dayton and Marta
Dietrich Edie.
*Courtesy Ross O. and
Doris J. Hockenbury.*

Clarence Michael Edie. Marta was naturalized as a United States citizen in San Francisco in 1952.

The Edie family was living in Valley Station, near Fort Knox, Kentucky, when Dayton retired from the army in 1965, and it became their permanent home. While Dayton worked at Jewish Hospital after he retired from the army, Marta found academic and cultural pursuits. In 1967 she received a bachelor of arts degree, *magna cum laude*, from Catherine Spalding College, and in 1971 she earned a master of arts degree from the University of Louisville. In 1968 she began teaching German classes as a part-time lecturer at the University of Louisville.

Following the tragic death of her son in 1976, Marta became more involved in teaching at the University of Louisville and was appointed to an assistant professorship in 1978. Professor Alan Leidner, one of Marta's colleagues in the German Department, recalled,

> *She was a lively presence whose courses, especially her theater practicum, had a dedicated following. She also taught courses on poetry, folklore, fairy tales, and (at least once) German humor. She and her student theater company produced numerous plays based on materials ranging from Goethe's* Faust *to children's literature. Her research dealt mainly with foreign language pedagogy, and she was one of several German faculty who directed the Mainz summer program that our department ran at the time.*

Marta retired from teaching in 1988, but thirty years later, her former students still speak glowingly of her courses and her abilities as a teacher.

In 1976 Louisville Mayor Harvey Sloane appointed a thirty-five-member citizens committee to revitalize Louisville's neglected sister city program. At the time, Louisville had only two sister cities—Montpelier, France, and Quito, Ecuador—and was actively searching for two more sister cities, with one in Germany. As a native German and a member of the University of Louisville's German faculty, Marta was involved with the committee. Initially, the city of Louisville approached Heidelberg, the home city of Marta's dear friend Ingeborg Reiter Holl. Unfortunately, Heidelberg already had sister city affiliations with two other U.S. cities and did not want to take on a third because of the costs involved.

At Marta's suggestion, Louisville turned to Mainz—a river city like Louisville with many common interests. Marta personally delivered an invitation from Mayor Sloane to Mainz Mayor Jockel Fuchs, who was enthused about the relationship but suggested "a further exchange of information before a decision is made." Thus began a long courtship of cultural exchanges between Mainz and Louisville, before a formal agreement was signed in 1994.

On the Louisville side, a Mainz sister city committee was set up, initially under the leadership of Marta Edie and with great assistance from Ingeborg Holl. On the Mainz side, a "Louisville Friendship Circle" was set up. The two groups organized student and medical faculty exchanges between Johannes Gutenberg University in Mainz and the University of Louisville as well as artist exchanges and business exchanges. In the early years of the Louisville-Mainz relationship, Marta Edie truly was the force that kept it alive and made it work. Today, the two most active Louisville sister city groups are the Mainz committee and the Montpelier committee.

Dayton Edie died quietly in his sleep on January 7, 2012, and Marta followed four years later on July 10, 2016.

ALBERT AND ELSIE GROTHEN GERRITS

Else (Elsie) Louise Grothen was born on July 9, 1924, in Fort Wayne, Indiana. Her parents, Friedrich (Fred) and Frieda Runge Grothen, immigrated to the United States from Achim, near Bremen, Germany, in 1923. The couple arrived at the Port of New York on November 11 aboard the ship *America*.

They were accompanied by a three-year-old son, Friedrich. The family settled in Fort Wayne, where Fred found employment as a typesetter for the *Freie Presse-Staats-Zeitung*, a German-language newspaper. A second daughter, Hedwiga (Hilda), was born to the Grothen family in 1925.

During the anti-German hysteria of World War I, all things German were suppressed, including German-language newspapers. Those that survived the war died a slow death afterward. Not surprisingly, the *Freie Presse* ceased publication in 1927.

Fred Grothen quickly secured employment as a typesetter for the *Louisville Anzeiger*, another German-language newspaper, and the Grothen family moved to Louisville. The *Louisville Anzeiger* was the longest-lived and preeminent German-language newspaper in Louisville. Founded in 1849, it began struggling in the 1930s and eventually ceased publication in 1938. Sensing the eventual demise of the *Anzeiger* and suffering the hard times of the Great Depression, Fred Grothen and his family returned to Germany in 1934.

Albert Ludwig Diedrich Gerrits was born in Achim on August 15, 1922. As a young man, he served in the German army during World War II. Following the war, he married Elsie Grothen in Achim on May 8, 1948. Their two sons, Friedrich and Werner, were born in Achim. The Gerrits family immigrated to the United States in 1952. They arrived at the Port of New York on May 7 aboard the ship *Gripsholm*. The family settled in Louisville, where Albert found employment as a bricklayer for Scheich and Taft Masonry Contractors. Albert Gerrits was naturalized as a United States citizen in 1962.

In 1953 Albert joined the Social Male Chorus, and Elsie joined the Ladies Auxiliary. The club afforded the Gerrits family the opportunity to enjoy the camaraderie of fellow German immigrants and to celebrate the culture of their homeland. Albert was the president of the club for fourteen years during the 1960s and 1970s and again in the 1990s. He was president when the club celebrated its 100th anniversary in 1978, and he is credited with starting the club's annual Oktoberfest celebration, which is a successful event that continues today.

Albert Gerrits. *Courtesy German-American Club Gesangverein.*

In 1965, Albert's first year as president, Urban Renewal forced the club to relocate from its home at 318 South Jackson Street to its present location at 1840 Lincoln Avenue. Albert and Gus Boeckmann, then the immediate past-president, worked together to plan the move and to secure the land for a new clubhouse. They and countless other club members built the new facility brick by brick.

In 1995 Albert Gerrits was nominated for and received the Bundesverdienstkreutz merit award from the Federal Republic of Germany. The award is given for "long outstanding and distinguished service in promoting relations between Germany and the United States." The award is given only sparingly, and it is a true honor. More than three hundred family members, friends and well-wishers were in attendance at the German-American Club (formerly the Social Male Chorus), where the presentation was made by Marianne Wannow, the consul general of the German Consulate in Detroit. The nomination was made by the Richmond, Virginia, branch of the Hauni Corporation, a German cigarette machine maker.

Albert Gerrits continued to serve the German-American Club in many ways until his death on November 12, 1997. His widow, Elsie, passed away on December 12, 2009.

LYDIA KÄSMANN HERRON

Lydia Käsmann was born on April 30, 1927, in the Zabo neighborhood of Nürnberg, to Martin and Anna Marie Scheuring Käsmann. As a young woman, she was a gifted athlete, competing for Germany in roller skating and ice skating, as well as excelling in track and field, water skiing and snow skiing. She was one of Germany's best figure skaters by age sixteen when she placed eighth in the 1943 European Championships. She would have been a contender for a spot on Germany's Olympic team in 1944, but the Olympics were not held because of World War II.

When interviewed by WAVE Television's John Boel in 2014, Lydia commented about the missed opportunity of the 1944 Olympics, "Nürnberg was burning for weeks after the bombings. My father was among those who were killed. My brother was deathly sick fighting on the Eastern Front, and my mother was sick too. There were more important things to worry about."

Following World War II, Lydia met Raymond "Leo" Herron, a U.S. Army serviceman, at the Casa Carioca Club in Garmisch. She was training with

Lydia Käsmann Herron. *Courtesy Trudy Herron Moneyhan.*

and competing for First FCN, a Nürnberg sports club, and later became a performer for the Casa Carioca ice show. A romance bloomed between Lydia and Leo, and they were married on October 10, 1947, in Bad Nauheim, near Frankfurt.

Leo Herron was born on May 5, 1921, in Clay, Webster County, Kentucky. He fought in World War II and was stationed in southern Germany with U.S. occupation forces after the war, when he met Lydia. After Leo and Lydia married, she immigrated to the United States via Pan American Airlines through Frankfurt to New York on November 25, 1947.

Leo and Lydia Käsmann Herron settled first in Clay, Kentucky, where their two children, Trudy and Steven, who died at birth, were born. Leo worked for a wholesale furniture company based in nearby Evansville, Indiana, and Lydia reared their daughter and taught roller skating in neighboring communities. Roberts Stadium in Evansville was being constructed at that time and planned to have an ice skating rink. Lydia secured a coaching job there and developed the skating program. To promote the program, the *Evansville Courier and Press* published a weekly column called Skating with Miss Lydia, which gave helpful skating hints.

The Herron family moved to Evansville about 1957, and Lydia was better able to manage the skating program at Roberts Stadium. While living there, another son, Erick, was born. Leo and Lydia were active members of the Germania Maennerchor, a German singing society in Evansville, and upon moving to Louisville, they joined the Social Male Chorus.

Leo and Lydia moved to Louisville in 1969, and Lydia became a skating instructor at the Gardiner Lane Ice Rink—later Alpine Ice Arena. About the same time, Robert Unger, a skating colleague of Lydia's at First FCN, also immigrated to the United States, eventually settling in Knoxville, Tennessee. He established the Robert Unger School of Ice Skating at the newly constructed Ice Chalet. He pioneered precision ice skating at a skilled level below professional skating. He and Lydia became prominent in the Ice Skating Institute of America, a body that promoted the development of ice skating rinks throughout the United States and contributed significantly to recreational figure skating.

Lydia taught at Gardiner Lane Ice Rink for thirty-seven years before retiring at age eighty in 2007. During her fifty years of instruction, she trained hundreds, if not thousands, of students, some achieving national status. She also coached many precision skating teams for competition and exhibitions.

One of Lydia's proudest accomplishments was her involvement with "Moms on Ice," a precision ice skating team for women over twenty-five. Moms on Ice was founded at Gardiner Lane in 1965 by Erika Amundsen. When Amundsen retired in 1989, Lydia became the coach. Moms on Ice exists today and participates in ice shows and competitions worldwide. Gardiner Lane (Alpine) celebrated its fiftieth anniversary three years after Lydia retired. On that occasion, Lydia remarked about Moms on Ice, "The greatest thing is to see people who thought they were too old to skate, then they see us go out there. It was unbelievable."

Leo Herron died on July 7, 1999. When Lydia finally retired, she remained active in the German-American Club (formerly the Social Male Chorus) and Sister Cities of Louisville, as well as a ladies' golf group and many social clubs and church groups. Lydia Käsmann Herron passed away on February 10, 2017, at age eighty-nine.

BIBLIOGRAPHY

Introduction

Cincinnati Enquirer. "Two Centuries on the Ohio River." 2012.

Louisville Daily Journal. "Reminiscences of an Old Connection with the *Louisville Journal*, Chapter XIII." November 27, 1867.

"Persons Obtaining Legal Permanent Resident Status by Region and Selected Country of Last Residence: Fiscal Years 1820 to 2010." *2010 Yearbook of Immigration Statistics*. Washington, D.C.: Office of Immigration Statistics, 2010.

Stierlin, Ludwig. *Der Staat Kentucky und die Stadt Louisville mit besonderer Berücksichtigung des deutschen Elementes*. Louisville: Anzeiger Press, 1873.

German Radicalism and the Forty-Eighters

Bogen, Frederick W. *The German in America*. Boston: B.H. Green, 1851.

Eyck, Frank, ed. *The Revolutions of 1848–49*. New York: Barnes and Noble Books, 1972.

Kranzberg, Melvin, ed. *1848: A Turning Point?* Boston: D.C. Heath and Company, 1959.

Lamier, Lewis. *1848: The Revolution of the Intellectuals*. Garden City, NY: Doubleday and Company, 1964.

Lewis, Hanna Ballin, ed. *A Year of Revolutions: Fanny Lewald's Recollections of 1848*. Providence, RI, and Oxford: Berghahn Books, 1997.

Tolzmann, Don Heinrich, ed. *The German-American Forty-Eighters, 1848–1849.* Indianapolis: Max Kade German-American Center, Indiana University–Purdue University Indianapolis, 1998.

Post–Civil War German Catholic Churches

Crews, Clyde F. *An American Holy Land: A History of the Archdiocese of Louisville.* Wilmington, DE: Michael Glazier Inc., 1987.
Louisville Courier-Journal. "Catholic Prelate Succumbs at Clinic." November 30, 1931.

The German Evangelisch Movement

Bethel-St. Paul Church, Louisville, KY. Parish Archives.
Schneider, Carl E. *The German Church on the American Frontier.* St. Louis, MO: Eden Publishing House, 1939.
St. John United Church of Christ. Louisville, KY. Parish Archives.
White, Terry L. *A Home for Children: A History of Brooklawn.* Edited by John E. Kleber. Louisville, KY: Montage Publishing Solutions Inc., 2001.

Financial Institutions

Allison, Young Ewing. *The City of Louisville and a Glimpse of Kentucky.* Louisville, KY: Committee on Industrial and Commercial Improvement of the Louisville Board of Trade, 1887.
Ernest Christian Bohné Memoir and Scrapbook, ca. 1870–1900. Special Collections Filson Historical Society, Louisville.
Johnston, J. Stoddard. "Insurance and Insurance Companies." In *Memorial History of Louisville from Its First Settlement to the Year 1896.* Vol. 1, edited by J. Stoddard Johnston, 304–8. New York: American Biographical Publishing Company, 1896.
Leathers, John H. "Banks and Banking Institutions." In *Memorial History of Louisville from Its First Settlement to the Year 1896.* Vol. 1, edited by J. Stoddard Johnston, 284–92. New York: American Biographical Publishing Company, 1896.

McCabe, James R. "Banking." In *The Encyclopedia of Louisville*, edited by John E. Kleber. Lexington: University Press of Kentucky, 2001.

Riebel, Raymond C. *Louisville Panorama: A Visual History of Louisville.* 3rd ed. Louisville, KY: Liberty National Bank and Trust Company, 1960.

Manufacturing

Falk, Gary. *Made in Louisville: Industrial Achievements of a Great American City from Its Founding to the Year 2013.* Shepherdsville, KY: Publishers Printing Company, 2013.

Friesen, Michael D. "The Prante Organbuilding Family." *Tracker: Journal of the Organ Historical Society* 37, no. 2 (1993): 8–17.

Hines, Philip T., Jr. "Pipe Organs." In *The Encyclopedia of Louisville*, edited by John E. Kleber. Lexington: University Press of Kentucky, 2001.

Jenkins-Evans, Holly. Past Perfect Vintage Clothing. "Louisville Department Stores: A Short History." 2013. http://pastperfectvintage.com/louisvillestores.htm.

"John Rohrman, the Ice King." In *Kentucky's Resources and Industries, Louisville.* Louisville: Railway Publishing Company, n.d.

Missouri Botanical Garden. "Women in Garden History." Catherine Martin. March 20, 2018. http://discoverandshare.org/2018/03/20/women-in-garden-history.

Rush, Dorothy C. "Ice Companies." In *The Encyclopedia of Louisville*, edited by John E. Kleber. Lexington: University Press of Kentucky, 2001.

Mineral Water, Soft Drinks, and the Municipal Water Supply

Crittenden, George A., ed. *The Industries of Louisville.* Louisville, KY: A.N. Marquis and Company, 1881.

Guetig, Peter R., and Conrad D. Selle. "Soft Drinks and Mineral Water." In *The Encyclopedia of Louisville*, edited by John E. Kleber. Lexington: University Press of Kentucky, 2001.

McMurtrie, Henry. *Sketches of Louisville and Its Environs.* Louisville, KY: S. Penn, 1819.

The Quest for Pure Water. Louisville, KY: Louisville Water Company, March 1, 2017.

Trades

Hanna, Hilton E., and Joseph Belsky. *Picket and the Pen: The "Pat" Gorman Story.* Yonkers, NY: American Institute of Social Science, 1960.

Hennen, John. "Toil, Trouble and Transformation: Workers and Unions in Modern Kentucky." *Register of the Kentucky Historical Society* 113 (Spring/Summer 2015): 233–69.

History of the Ohio Falls Cities and their Counties. Cleveland, OH: L.A. Williams and Company, 1882.

Louisville Courier-Journal. "Gambrinus Cooperage Works." June 26, 1933.

———. "Marvelous Growth." September 2, 1887.

Louisville Daily Courier. Bee Hive Gallery advertisement. November 10, 1858.

Medicine

Garrison, R. Neal, and Lewis Flint. "Establishing the Principles of Civilian and Military Injury Care: Samuel David Gross at the University of Louisville, 1840–1856." *Journal of the American College of Surgery* 210 (May 2010): e1–e8.

Hafner, Arthur W., ed. *Directory of Deceased American Physicians, 1804–1929.* Chicago: American Medical Association, 1993.

Landau, Herman. *Adath Louisville: The Story of a Jewish Community.* Louisville, KY: Herman Landau and Associates, 1981.

Louisville Courier-Journal. "German Celebration at Phoenix Hill Park This Evening." November 10, 1889.

Louisville Daily Journal. "Reminiscences of an Old Connection with *The Louisville Journal,* Chapter XIII." November 27, 1867.

Mathews, Joseph M. "Medicine and Medical Institutions." In *The Memorial History of Louisville from Its First Settlement to the Year 1896.* Vol. 1, edited by J. Stoddard Johnston. New York City: American Biographical Publishing Company, 1896.

Stierlin, Ludwig. *Der Staat Kentucky und die Stadt Louisville mit besonderer Berücksichtigung des deutschen Elementes.* Louisville: Anzeiger Press, 1873.

Legal Arts

Beckner, Lucien. "History of the County Court of Lincoln County, Virginia." *Register of Kentucky State Historical Society* 20 (May 1922): 170–190.

Levin, H., ed. *The Lawyers and Lawmakers of Kentucky.* Chicago: The Lewis Publishing Company, 1897.

Louisville Courier-Journal. "Lewis Naphtali Dembitz." February 27, 1916.

———. "Louisville Women Invade Men's Field." November 21, 1920.

———. "Muir Weissinger, 82, Former County Judge, Dies." August 2, 1952.

———. "O.A. Wehle, Attorney, Dies in City At 85." January 2, 1931.

Sallee, Helen Hite. "The Descendants of Colonel Abraham Hite." *Kentucky Ancestors* 7 (April 1971): 186–92.

Southard, Mary Young, and Ernest C. Miller, eds. *Who's Who in Kentucky: A Biographical Assembly of Notable Kentuckians.* Louisville, KY: Standard Print, 1936.

Urofsky, Melvin I. *Louis D. Brandeis: A Life.* New York: Pantheon Books, 2009.

Fine Arts

Bier, Justus. "Carl C. Brenner: A German-American Landscapist." *The American-German Review* 17 (April 1951): 20–4.

Brenner, Henry, OSB. "My Old Kentucky Home." 1921. Unpublished memoir held by St. Meinrad Archabbey, St. Meinrad, Indiana.

"Joseph Krementz." In *The Encyclopedia of Louisville*, edited by John E. Kleber. Lexington: University Press of Kentucky, 2001.

Louisville Courier-Journal. "Nicola Marschall's Memory Shared Across the Sea." July 6, 1958.

———. "Noted Artist Is Dead at 88." February 24, 1917.

Miller, Chris. "Paul Albert Plaschke." *This Old Palette.* Palette and Chisel Art Academy, March 30, 2011. thisoldpalette.blogspot.com.

Montgomery Advertiser. "Alabama Hails Nicola Marschall as Designer of Confederate Flag." June 2, 1931.

Paul A. Plaschke. Personal papers of Paul A, Plaschke held by Paul S. Plaschke Jr., Louisville, KY.

Music

Hall of Honor Biography. "Gerhard Herz (1911–2000)." University of Louisville, College of Arts and Sciences. 2010. http://louisville.edu/artsandsciences/about/hallofhonor/inductees/gerhard-herz.

Kramer, Mary Kagin. "Louisville Bach Society." In *The Encyclopedia of Louisville*, edited by John E. Kleber. Lexington: University Press of Kentucky, 2001.

Louisville Courier-Journal. "'Papa' Karl Schmidt, Much-Loved Cellist and Composer of Louisville, Dies at 86." October 8, 1950.

———. "Prof. Hast's Self-Murder." February 13, 1890.

Woolsey, Frederick William. "Heinrich Hans Claus Moritz von Bomhard." In *The Encyclopedia of Louisville*, edited by John E. Kleber. Lexington: University Press of Kentucky, 2001.

Wuest, John B., OFM. *One Hundred Years of St. Boniface Parish, Louisville, Kentucky: A Historical Sketch.* Louisville, KY: George G. Fetter Company, 1937.

Yater, George H. *Two Hundred Years at the Falls of the Ohio.* Louisville, KY: The Filson Club, 1987.

Germans in Southern Indiana

Amster, Betty Lou. *New Albany on the Ohio: Historical Review, 1813–1963.* New Albany, IN: New Albany Sesquicentennial Incorporated, 1963.

Kramer, Carl E. "Jeffersonville, Indiana." In *The Encyclopedia of Louisville*, edited by John E. Kleber. Lexington: University Press of Kentucky, 2001.

———. "New Albany." In *The Encyclopedia of Louisville*, edited by John E. Kleber. Lexington: University Press of Kentucky, 2001.

———. *This Place We Call Home: A History of Clark County, Indiana.* Bloomington: Indiana University Press, 2017.

Portraits of Twentieth Century Immigrants

Louisville Courier-Journal. "Alpine Arena Glides into 50." September 22, 2010.

———. "Deutsche Treat." July 26, 1995.

———. "Louisville is Trying to Get Two New 'Sisters.'" March 1, 1977.

"Talented German Skater Has No Regrets About Missing Olympics during WWII." WAVE Television News, Louisville, KY. 2014. http://www.wave3.com/story/24667457/hitler-youth-skater-has-no-regrets-at-what-might-have-been.

INDEX

ABOUT THE AUTHORS

C. Robert Ullrich and Victoria A. Ullrich, editors. *Courtesy Paolo De Caro.*

KEVIN COLLINS is the author of more than fifty articles on law, civil liberties and Kentucky history for five encyclopedias and one magazine.

GARY FALK is a historian, author of *Louisville Remembered* (2009) and *Made in Louisville* (2013) and author of "Music" in *The Encyclopedia of Louisville* (2001) as well as "Louisville Musical History" in *The New Grove Dictionary of Music and Musicians* (2013).

PETER R. GUETIG is the co-author of *Louisville Breweries: A History of the Brewing Industry in Louisville, Kentucky, New Albany, and Jeffersonville, Indiana* (2014) and *Louisville Dairies* (2016) as well as "Soft Drinks and Mineral Water" in *The Encyclopedia of Louisville* (2001).

KATHERINE BURGER JOHNSON is a retired associate professor, Kornhauser Health Sciences Library, University of Louisville, as well as the author of *Juniper, That's Me* (1995), a chapter in *Personal Perspectives, World War I* and more than fifteen encyclopedia entries on Louisville and women in the military.

JOHN E. KLEBER, PhD, is a professor emeritus of history at Morehead State University, as well as the editor of six books, including *The Kentucky Encyclopedia* (1992) and *The Encyclopedia of Louisville* (2001).

F. RICHARD KNOOP is a German teacher, German club moderator and chorus moderator at St. Xavier High School, as well as the music minister at St. Frances of Rome Catholic Church.

CARL E. KRAMER, PhD, is the retired director of the Institute for Local and Oral History, adjunct assistant professor of history at Indiana University Southeast and author of thirteen books about the history of the Louisville Metropolitan area.

MICHAEL E. MALONEY is the Field Research Director, Community Relations and Events for the Louisville Mayor's Office.

R. CHARLES MOYER, PhD, is a professor of finance and entrepreneurship in the College of Business at the University of Louisville, as well as the author of four textbooks on finance and management.

KATHLEEN PELLEGRINO is the former vice president and deputy general counsel of Humana, Inc.

WILLIAM C. SCHRADER, PhD, is a professor emeritus of history at Tennessee Technological University.

REVEREND GORDON A. SEIFFERTT is a retired UCC minister and authority on German Evangelical and Reformed churches in Louisville.

CONRAD D. SELLE is the co-author of *Louisville Breweries: A History of the Brewing Industry in Louisville, Kentucky, New Albany, and Jeffersonville, Indiana* (2014) and *Louisville Dairies* (2016) as well as "Soft Drinks and Mineral Water" in *The Encyclopedia of Louisville* (2001).

ABOUT THE AUTHORS

PATRICIA BOECKMANN STOUT is the assistant controller and treasury manager for Midwest Metals Corporation and past president of the German-American Club, Gesangverein.

DAVID P. TAYLOR is an antiques and fine arts dealer and collector and owner of David P. Taylor Antiques in Owensboro, Kentucky, specializing in Kentucky art and regional furniture.

C. ROBERT ULLRICH, PhD, is a professor emeritus of civil and environmental engineering at the University of Louisville. He is also the co-editor of *Germans in Louisville: A History* (2015) and the co-author of "Germans" in *The Encyclopedia of Louisville* (2001).

VICTORIA A. ULLRICH is the past president of the Germanic Heritage Auxiliary, German-American Club Gesangverein, and the co-editor of *Germans in Louisville: A History* (2015).

Visit us at
www.historypress.com